בס"ד

The Garden of Yearning

A wonderfully inspiring interpretation
of Rebbe Nachman's Tale, "The Lost Princess"

By
Rabbi Shalom Arush

Director of "Chut shel Chessed" Institutions
Author of "The Garden of Emuna" and other books

Translated by:

Rabbi Lazer Brody

Elul, 5767

In all matters relating to this book, please contact:

publications@lazerbrody.net

Distribution:
Tel: 972-52-2240696

www.breslov.co.il
www.breslovworld.com

ISBN: 978-0-9798840-0-9

Design and Layout:
Eye See Productions
972-2-5821453

Printed in Israel

Published in cooperation with

munah
Outreach

Table of Contents

Translator's Foreword

Rabbi Shalom Arush's first English-translated book, **The Garden of Emuna,** made its debut less than a year ago. It's hard to imagine any other contemporary work that has had such a monumental impact the world over, from Australia to Alaska and all points in between, in such a short time. His golden message has opened up new gateways of hope and happiness to tens of thousands of people. As one reader wrote me, "My life is divided into two parts – before I read The Garden of Emuna and after I read **The Garden of Emuna.**" Anything more is superfluous.

Rabbi Shalom's words are a cool drink to a parched soul. He – like our teacher and master Rebbe Nachman of Breslov of blessed and saintly memory - is a master physician of the soul who adeptly cures all people's ills with one secret spiritual remedy – *emuna*, the pure and complete faith in The Almighty.

With Hashem's loving grace, I've had the privilege of maintaining a close relationship with Rabbi Shalom Arush for over a decade already, both as the dean of the Ashdod branch of his renowned rabbinical seminary, "Chut Shel Chessed" and as his English translator and understudy. More than anyone I've ever seen, Rabbi Shalom meticulously practices what he preaches. He is the undisputed pillar of emuna in this generation.

The problem with **The Garden of Emuna** is that it left readers yearning for more. A reader from Washington State wrote, "Now what do I do? I've finished your amazing book and I need more. I can't pack up and move to Jerusalem to enroll in your Yeshiva, so please don't leave me hanging. I need more guidance and more emuna!"

Rabbi Shalom is not one to rest on his laurels. He works day and night, learning, teaching, lecturing, writing, and spreading emuna wherever he goes. Sometimes, days go by without his head meeting a pillow. Before I had the opportunity to discuss with him the need of a sequel to **The Garden of Emuna**, the original Hebrew *B'gan HaGa'aguim* was already half written.

B'gan HaGa'aguim, known in English as **The Garden of Yearning**, is an amazing interpretation of Rebbe Nachman's tale, "The Lost Princess." Rabbi Shalom penetrates the inner dimension of this poignant allegory to extract Rebbe Nachman's instructional allusions to emuna and to the proper way of serving Hashem, thus attaining true fulfillment in life. This book is not for the spiritual novice, but for the individual that yearns for and seeks a stronger connection with Hashem. This book is most beneficial after one reads **The Garden of Emuna** carefully, from cover to cover.

With Hashem's loving guidance, I have tried my utmost to preserve the flavor and intent of Rabbi Shalom's original style. I have taken no license in translating Rebbe Nachman's holy words in the "Tale of the Lost Princess," not even for the sake of accepted English grammar and syntax, since Rav Shalom Arush's inspiring interpretations are based on these precise words. Even so, any deficiency in this book is surely that of the translator and not of the author. My sincere thanks and blessings go to Rachel Tzipporah Salkover and to Rivka Levy for their dedicated assistance in editing and proofreading.

I wish to express my deepest gratitude to Rabbi Shalom Arush himself, who so selflessly has illuminated my mind and soul with his noble teachings. May Hashem bless him, his family, and his pupils with the very best of spiritual and material abundance always.

My cherished wife Yehudit deserves the credit for this book and for everything else I do. May Hashem bless her with long and happy days, success, and joy from all her offspring. May they walk courageously in the path of Torah and emuna until the end of time, amen.

With a song of thanks to the Almighty and a prayer for the full and speedy redemption of our people Israel,

Rabbi Lazer Brody, Ashdod, Elul 5767

Author's Foreword

slight mention

Dear Reader,

Awesome secrets are concealed within the tales of our holy Rebbe Nachman of Breslov, of which we have no concept; his allusions are numerous and deeper than the sea. One can attempt to interpret them according to one's own level of comprehension.

This book results from my traditional Shabbat talk following morning services, when we study of **Rebbe Nachman's Tales**, as is the custom in all Breslover communities. My nuances from these talks glow in the light of the Shabbat and in the light of the holy *tzaddik* and his disciples, whose words are intertwined in every page. *variation*

We've attempted to arrange this book in a reader-friendly manner. Rebbe Nachman's original words appear in easily recognizable form, and for the readers' benefit, we've placed the original tale at the beginning of the book and a glossary in the back of the book.

Those who are familiar with the content of "The Lost Princess" can derive from it a wealth of wisdom when seeing the amazing way that awesome messages of emuna and spiritual reinforcement are hinted in Rebbe Nachman's words. From one standpoint, the tale is utter simplicity; on the other hand, it's a kaleidoscopic tool that's beneficial to all people on all rungs of the spiritual ladder.

How shall I thank Hashem for all His loving-kindness? If my mouth was as full of praise as the waters of the ocean, I couldn't thank Hashem for even one of the hundreds of thousands of millions of miracles and wonders that He has done for me, enabling me to delight in the sweet allusions that our holy Rebbe Nachman has left by way of these wonderful tales: They illuminate the world with simple faith while strengthening the path of *teshuva*, joy, and love.

My first blessings go out to my teacher and spiritual guide, Rabbi Eliezer Berland shlit'a; may it be Hashem's will that he enjoy long and fruitful days leading us, and may he continue on his wonderful way of raising pupils and pupils of pupils, while blessed with strength of body and with illumination from above.

My heartfelt thanks to my mother and teacher, Yamna bat Esther, may Hashem grant her length of days. May she derive limitless gratification from all of her children and offspring, and may she live to see the illumination of Moshiach's countenance, may he come soon.

A special thanks to my dedicated wife, a blessed woman of valor, Miriam Varda, may Hashem grant her length of days. She is my friend, partner, help, and source of everything good. All my success and everything I have are in her merit and belong to her. May we continue together to see the success of our offspring and of all of our pupils, and the full redemption of Israel speedily and in our days.

My faithful friend and pupil, Rabbi Eliezer Raphael (Lazer) Brody, may Hashem guard over him, translator of this book and author of "Pi HaBe'er", "Nafshi Tidom", and "The Trail to Tranquility", has tirelessly dedicated himself to spreading my teachings. His translation and adaptation of **The Garden of Emuna** and of my CD lessons have already spread in the tens of thousands to every continent on the globe. May Hashem grant him strength, success, and joy from his offspring, and may we continue together to spread emuna in the world until the age of 120.

Last but not least are my dear pupils Rabbi Yaakov Hertzberg and his wife Esther, may Hashem bless them, who have merited from above in assisting me with the composition of my books. May Hashem bless them with long and happy days, and may they see success from their children and the light of emuna – which they help spread – illuminate the world and their path in life.

May it be Your will, Father in Heaven, that all of Israel walks in the path of *teshuva*, love, and truth, and may Your glorious kingdom be revealed on earth speedily, amen.

Rabbi Shalom Arush, Jerusalem, Elul 5767

favorable opinion

Approbations

quotes

The following are excerpts from the approbations that this generation's leading rabbinical figures wrote for the original Hebrew version of **The Garden of Yearning**:

Rabbi Ovadia Yossef, Rishon Letzion and President of the Counsel of Torah Sages:

"**The Garden of Yearning** is the work of an artist, the Prince of Torah, the brilliant and pious Rabbi Shalom Arush, may he merit long and happy days, who has assembled in his purity a golden treasure of wonderful spiritual arousal..." *stir to action*

Grand Rabbi Naftali Moscowitz, the Melitzer Rebbe:

"The Divine Presence glistens from the pages of **The Garden of Yearning,** which is full of spiritual arousal and practical advice for the strengthening of emuna in everyday life, all derived from reliable sources that walk in the path of holiness... Every person will derive benefit from this book, for there is no limit to the obligation to learn and relearn about emuna until it becomes internalized in the heart..."

Rabbi Eliezer Berland, Rosh Yeshiva of Shuvu Banim Breslov, Jerusalem:

"I read breathtakingly the holy and fabulous book **The Garden of Yearning** that will open the eyes of any person no matter where he is...the fountains of wisdom and understanding will open to whoever learns this book with earnest...anyone who contributes gold from his pocket to spread this book will merit seeing Moshiach and the rebuilding of our Holy Temple, amen!"

Tale of the Lost Princess

He answered and said: Along the way, I told a tale, that everyone who heard it had thoughts of repentance. And here it is...

There once was a king, who had six sons and one daughter. This daughter was very precious to him. He loved her exceptionally, and took great delight in her. Once time, he met with her on a certain day and he lost his temper at her, and an utterance escaped his mouth: "May the no-good-one take you!" In the evening she went to her room, and in the morning, no one knew where she was. Her father became very distraught, and he went everywhere looking for her.

The viceroy stood up, for he saw that the king was very troubled, and asked that he [the king – LB] provide him [the viceroy – LB] with a servant, a horse, and money for the journey, and set out to ask for her. He asked exhaustingly for a very long time, until he found her. (And following is the account of how he asked for her, until he found her). He went from place to place, for a very long time, in deserts, fields and forests. And he asked for her a very long time. As he was crossing a desert, he saw a path to the side, and he was composing himself: "Seeing that I've been going such a long time in the desert and I cannot find her, I'll try this path - maybe I'll come to a settled area." And he went a very long time on that path.

Afterwards, he saw a castle, with several soldiers standing guard around it. The castle was very attractive, well-built, and extremely orderly with the guards posted, and he was worried that the guards would not let him in. But he composed himself and said, "I will go and try." So he left the horse behind, and approached the castle. And the guards ignored him and did not hinder him. He went from room to room without disturbance, and came to one reception hall, where the king sat, wearing his crown. And there were a number of guards, and musicians with their instruments standing before him. It was all very pleasant and beautiful, and neither the king nor any of the others asked him anything at all.

followed

And he saw there delicacies and fine foods, and he stood and ate and went to lie down in a corner, to see what would transpire there. He saw that the king summoned for the queen. They went to bring her, and there ensued a great commotion and joy. The musicians played and sang a great deal, in that they were bringing the queen. They placed a chair for her and sat her next to the king. And she was the above-mentioned princess, and he (the viceroy) saw and recognized her.

After that, the queen gazed about and saw a man lying in a corner, and recognized him. She stood up from her chair and went over to him, nudging him, and asked him, "Do you recognize me?" He answered, "Yes, I do. You're the lost princess." And he asked her, "How did you get here?" She answered, "Because my father blurted out the words `The no good one should take you', and here, this place, is no good."

So he told her that her father is very sorry, and has been searching for several years. And he asked, "How can I get you out of here?" And she answered, "It's impossible for you to get me out of here unless you choose a place, and dwell there a full year. And the whole year, you must yearn to take me out. Any free time that you have, you should only yearn and pray and hope to free me. And you should fast frequently, and on the last day of the year, you should fast and not sleep the entire day." So he went and did just that.

something desired in sight

On the last day of the year, he fasted, and did not sleep, and rose and began the journey back [to the castle where the lost princess was held – LB]. And on the way he saw a tree, and on it grew very appealing apples. And they were irresistibly tantalizing to his eyes, so he approached and ate one. Right after eating the apple, he dropped and fell asleep, and he slept a very long time. His servant would try to wake him, but to no avail. Afterwards, he awoke from his sleep, and asked the servant, "Where am I in the world?" And the servant told him the story: "You were sleeping a very long time, several years. And I survived on the fruit." And he [the viceroy – LB] was very remorseful about hearing this.

So he returned there and found her. And she revealed her great distress to him. "If you had only come on the prescribed day, you would have taken me out of here. And because of one day, you lost. Nevertheless, it is very difficult not to eat, especially on the last day, when the Evil Inclination is very overpowering. (In other words, the princess told him that now she would make the conditions more lenient, that from now he would not be expected to fast, for that is a very hard condition to fulfill, etc.) So now, choose a place again, and dwell there also a year, as before. And on the last day you will be allowed to eat. Only you must not sleep, and must not drink wine, so you won't fall asleep. For the essential thing is not to sleep." So he went and did accordingly.

color

On the last day, he would go there, and saw a spring flowing, with a reddish hue and a wine-scented fragrance. He asked the servant, "Did you see that spring, which should have water in it, but its color is red, and its scent is of wine?" And he [the viceroy – LB] went and sipped from the spring. And he immediately fell into a sleep that lasted several years - seventy, to be exact. And great numbers of soldiers passed by with their accompanying gear. The servant hid himself from the soldiers. Afterwards came a covered carriage, and in it sat the princess. She stopped next to him [the viceroy – LB]. She descended and sat by him, recognizing who he was. She shook him strongly, but he failed to wake up. And she started to bemoan, "How many immense efforts and travails he has undergone, these many years, in order to free me, and because of one day that he could have freed me, and lost it...," and she cried a great deal about this, saying "There is great pity for him and for me, that I am here so very long, and cannot leave." After that, she took her scarf off of her head, and wrote upon it with her tears, and laid it by him. And she rose and boarded her carriage, and rode away. Afterwards, he [the viceroy – LB] awoke, and asked the servant, "Where am I in the world?" So he [the servant – LB] told him the whole story - that many soldiers had passed there, and that there had been a carriage, and a woman who wept over him and cried out that there is great pity on him and on her. In the midst of this, he [the viceroy – LB] looked around and saw that there was a scarf lying next to him. So he asked, "Where did this come from?" The servant explained that she had written upon it with her tears. So he took it and held it up against the sun, and began to see the letters, and he read all that was written there - all her mourning and crying as previously mentioned, and that she is no longer in the said castle, and that he should look for a mountain of gold and a castle of pearls, "There you shall find me!"

So he left the servant behind, and went to look for her alone. And he went for several years searching, and he composed himself, thinking that certainly a mountain of gold and a castle of pearls would not be found in a settled area, for he was an expert in the map of the world. So he went to the deserts. And he searched for her there many years.

Afterwards, he saw a giant man, far beyond the normal human proportions. He was carrying a massive tree, the size of which is not found in settled areas. The man asked him, "Who are you?" He answered, "I am a man." The giant was amazed, and exclaimed, "I have been in the desert such a long time, and I have never seen a man here." So he [the viceroy – LB] told him the whole story, and that he was searching for a mountain of gold and a castle of pearls. The giant answered him, "Certainly, it does not exist at all." And he [the giant – LB] discouraged him and said that they had muddled his mind with nonsense, for it surely does not exist. So he (the viceroy) started to cry bitterly, for he felt certain that it must exist somewhere. And this giant discouraged him, saying that certainly he had been told nonsense. Yet he (the viceroy) still said that it must exist.

So the giant said to him, "I think it is nonsense. But since you persist, I am in charge of the animals. I will do this for you: I will call them all. For they traverse the whole world, perhaps one of them will know where the mountain and the castle are." And he called them all, from the smallest to the largest, all the varieties of animals, and asked them. And all of them answered that they had not seen these things. So he said, "You see that they told you nonsense. If you want my advice, turn back, because you certainly will not find it, for it does not exist." And he [the viceroy – LB] pleaded passionately with him, saying, "But it absolutely must exist!" So the giant said to him, "Behold, in this desert also lives my brother, and he is in charge of the birds. Perhaps they know, since they fly at great heights - perhaps they saw this mountain and castle. Go to him and tell him that I sent you to him."

So he [the viceroy – LB] searched for him [the giant's brother – LB] for several years. And again he found a very large man, as before. He was also carrying a massive tree, as before. And this giant also asked him as had the first. And he [the viceroy – LB] told him the whole story, and that his brother had sent him to him. This giant also discouraged him, saying that it certainly did not exist. And he pleaded with him as with the first. Then the giant said to him, "Behold, I am in charge of the birds; I will call them, perhaps they know." So he called all the birds, and asked them all, from the smallest to the largest, and they answered that they did not know anything about this mountain and castle. So the giant said to him, "You see, it certainly does not exist. If you want my advice, turn back, for it simply does not exist." But he pleaded with him, saying "It certainly exists!"

The second giant said to him, "Further ahead in the desert lives my brother, who is in charge of the winds, and they run around the whole world. Perhaps they know." So he went several more years searching, and found also this giant, who was also carrying a giant tree. And the giant asked him, as the others had. And he told him the whole story, as before. And the giant discouraged him, as before. And he pleaded with him as well. So the third giant said to him, that for his sake he would call all the winds and ask them. He called them, and all the winds came, and he asked them all, and not one of them knew about the mountain and the castle. So the giant said to him, "You see, they told you nonsense." And the viceroy began to cry bitterly, and said, "I *know* that it certainly exists!"

As they were speaking, one more wind came. And the giant in charge of them was annoyed with him, saying, "Why did you not come with the rest?" He answered, "I was delayed, for I needed to carry a princess to a mountain of gold and a castle of pearls." And the viceroy was overjoyed. The one in charge asked the wind, "What is expensive there? (In other words, what things are considered valuable and important there?)" He [the wind – LB] answered him, "Everything there is extremely expensive." So the one in charge of the winds said to the viceroy, "Seeing that you have been searching for her such a long time, and you went through many difficulties. Perhaps now you will be hindered by expenses. Therefore I am giving you this vessel. Every time you reach into it, you will receive money from it." And he [the third giant – LB] commanded the aforementioned wind to take him [the viceroy – LB] there. The storm wind came, and carried him there, and brought him to the gate. There were guards posted there, that would not let him enter the city. So he reached into the vessel, took out money and bribed them, and entered the city. And it was a beautiful city.

He approached a man, and rented lodgings, for he would need to stay there some time. For it would need much cunning and wisdom to free her. And how he freed her, he [Rebbe Nachman – LB]did not tell, but in the end he freed her.

Chapter One

New Beginnings

He answered and said: Along the way, I told a tale, that everyone who heard it had thoughts of repentance. And here it is...

Before our holy Rebbe began telling this tale, he revealed that it would be capable of stimulating thoughts of repentance in anyone that heard it.

What are Thoughts of Repentance?

A thought of repentance is one's pondering in his or her heart that, "Even though I'm the most evil person in the universe, from this moment on, I want to change my ways and walk in the straight path according to Hashem's will."

The *Gemara* says – and Jewish religious law stipulates – that **as soon as a person has a thought of repentance, he or she is deemed a perfect *tzaddik*!** Even though a person has not yet actively performed a single mitzvah, and the only change in his or her life has been an invisible inner desire – Hashem gazes deep into that person's heart and mind and clearly sees their desire to change for the better. From that moment on, Hashem regards that person as a pious individual.

As long as we maintain the desire for repentance, or *teshuva*, Hashem continues to regard us as righteous individuals, even though we're still far from realizing our goals. Indeed, even if we're not yet working to improve our character - and we're still full of bad habits and bodily lusts with no idea whatsoever about the Hashem's ways and basic religious law – despite all this, if we cultivate an unequivocal desire is to improve ourselves, then Hashem considers regards us as complete *tzaddikim*. In any event, the road to spiritual improvement should be measured, gradual, and in accordance with proper instruction.

The above concept is a wonderful source of advice and encouragement for all of us. Even when we fall or fail, we can strengthen ourselves with a renewed resolve that from this moment on, we desire to walk in the path of righteousness. We must be courageous that no matter what, we'll never abandon our desire to be better and remain steadfast in our yearning to get close to Hashem and to do His will. As long as we cling to our aspirations of enhanced proximity to Hashem, Hashem continues to regard us as complete *tzaddikim*. As such, we benefit from Divine assistance in everything we do. Hashem's blessing and assistance enable us to succeed in all of our endeavors.

A Huge Benefit

When we never give up our desire and yearning to be better, we benefit in the following ways:

1. We literally work wonders with our prayers. Since Hashem and the Heavenly Court consider us tzaddikim, our prayers are always accepted.

2. Rebbe Nachman of Breslov says that desire is the main thing. Therefore, when we cultivate our desire to serve Hashem, we are doing what we're supposed to do. As such, we are assured of receiving a tikkun, or soul correction, in all of our actions, because our sages promise that Hashem will help us in the path we choose for ourselves.

3. When we learn the value of desire, we realize that a mere thought of *teshuva*, such as, "I want to do what Hashem wants me to do" is enough to alter a person's status from evil to righteous. This knowledge prevents us from becoming discouraged if we slip and fall, for all we have to do is to renew our resolve to serve Hashem with all our hearts, and we're back on our feet again!

Even if we fall or fail over and over again - and it's clear that we won't change overnight - we should never abandon our desires.

As long as the flame of desire to get closer to Hashem flickers in our hearts, Hashem continues to regard us as righteous. Hashem judges us not so much according to where we are, but according to where we want to go. The desire in our hearts overrules our actions. Hashem knows that personal improvement is a long hard road, but He regards us as *tzaddikim* the minute we begin our journey of yearning to be better.

4. Rebbe Nachman of Breslov writes (Likutei Moharan, I: 261): "When a person falls from his spiritual level, the best advice is to start anew in the service of Hashem, as if he never served Hashem in his life. For a person must strengthen himself in the service of Hashem and not to be discouraged by anything in the world, only declare a new beginning each time." When we know that our desire to serve Hashem earns us the status of *tzaddikim*, we can summon the inner strength to begin anew, even after the most disastrous fall or failure.

stir to action

Chapter Two

Emuna

T here once was a king, who had six sons and one daughter. This daughter was very precious to him. He loved her exceptionally, and took great delight in her...

Rebbe Nachman tells a tale of a king that had seven children – six sons and a daughter. A parent naturally loves a child, so the king most certainly loved his six sons. But, his daughter was special, so he loved her most of all. The king's daughter alludes to *emuna*, the pure and complete faith in Hashem. Rebbe Nachman always emphasized that the most important thing in our lives is emuna. Allegorically, even though there are many things that The King (Hashem) likes, He favors emuna more than anything else.

We should know that emuna is in itself one of Hashem's creations, as Rebbe Nachman writes (Likutei Moharan I: 173): "The soul and emuna are one aspect. There is a spiritual world of emuna, from where the characteristic of emuna is taken, **and the world of emuna itself has emuna in Hashem, blessed be He.**"

Throughout the entire Torah and throughout all of creation, we see that the number seven is the foundation of all things. Repeatedly, we see "six plus one" as an allusion to perfection. This is also an indication of emuna, for the number seven alludes to the perfection of every detail within creation.

Let's look at a few examples:

According to Kabbala, the world is governed by the seven lower spiritual spheres, and the seventh is *malchut*, or monarchy. The other six spheres all influence *malchut*, on which is dependant the *tikkun* of the entire universe. Each sphere has its own characteristic trait; *malchut's* characteristic trait is emuna.

The world was created in six days, and on the seventh day, Hashem declared a day of rest. Our sages learn creation earned its perfection by virtue of the Sabbath, the day of rest. Therefore, a week is divided into six days of handiwork, and the seventh day which is the "Sabbath Queen," the perfection and ultimate purpose of the entire week. The Sabbath is emuna.

The years are divided into six years where one tills the land, and the seventh year which is the *shmitta*, or Sabbatical year, when the land is allowed to rest. The *shmitta* year is totally dependent on emuna – when the farmer believes that Hashem will provide for him even though he's not growing anything that year. Seven cycles of seven years lead to an additional *yovel*, or Jubilee year, which is also a year that depends on emuna, for the land lies idle during the Jubilee year as well.

Seven planets govern the constellations, or the signs, of the zodiac. Emuna perfects the zodiac, as Rebbe Nachman of Breslov writes (Likutei Moharan I:31): "There is no perfection of the zodiac, other than emuna."

Seven days of mourning correct the deceased person's blemished emuna. The seven days that a leper must remain outside the encampment, the seven days of purification for one that has come in contact with a dead body, the seven days of *nidda*, the impure part of a woman's ovulation cycle, and the seven days of *kiddushin*, or betrothal, are all designed to correct and perfect emuna.

A slave serves his master for six years, and goes free in the seventh, for this is the correction of the blemished emuna that led to slavery in the first place.

There are seven openings in a person's face, all of which we must sanctify: two eyes, two ears, two nostrils, and the mouth; these correspond to the seven branches of the holy menorah, or candelabra in the *Beit Hamikdash*, our holy temple. We call these the seven candles, and we sanctify these seven candles by way of emuna.

All three Jewish festivals rotate around the theme of seven: Succoth is seven days; Passover is seven days; and Shavuot, which is only one day, but has seven days for one to fulfill the obligation of bringing a ritual sacrifice in the Holy Temple. Jewish esoteric thought teaches that the perfection of the festivals is by virtue of emuna.

The Oral Torah is based on seven – the six orders of the Mishna and the seventh, which is prayer.

The Seven Shepherds of our people – Abraham, Isaac, Jacob, Moses, Aaron, Joseph, and David – are the essence and root of our leaders in every generation, for they are the guardians of emuna as Rebbe Nachman explains (see Likutei Moharan I: 22).

There are seven parts of the world, seven climatic zones, seven source metals, seven types of wisdom, seven core character traits, and seven types of houses of idolatry. The eye is comprised of seven main parts. Spiritually, there are seven sounds, seven types of logical rebuttal, seventy faces of Torah, seventy sacrificial bulls during Succoth, and seven preparatory days before the inauguration of the holy Tabernacle, or *mishkan*. The Torah is full of many more sevens, all indicating the spiritual perfection attained via emuna.

In general, the number seven is *malchut*, or in other words, the characteristic of emuna. Emuna perfects everything, for we learn (see Abridged Likutei Moharan, I: 31): "The perfection of everything is emuna, and without emuna, everything is deficient. The perfection of Torah is only by way of emuna, for the Torah is based on emuna, since the main thing is emuna." We also learn there that "Emuna is the source of all blessings, and via emuna, all blessings are fulfilled." Rebbe Nathan of Breslov also says (Likutei Halachot, Hilchot Nidda, 2), that emuna is the vessel that holds the illuminations of all the world's *tikkunim*, or rectifications. Therefore, all the abovementioned sevens attain their perfection by way of emuna.

Precious, Loved, and Delightful

Rebbe Nachman uses three terms to describe the king's affection for the princess: "This daughter was very **precious** to him. He **loved** her exceptionally, and took great **delight** in her." These three terms all refer to emuna.

Precious – emuna is more precious to Hashem than anything that the world tends to consider valuable, rare, or important. For example, people give high regard to a scholar. But, if the scholar lacks emuna, he loses his stature, for Rebbe Nathan says specifically (see Abridged Likutei Moharan, I: 31): "A scholar alone (without emuna), is surely nothing, for one can be a scholar and an evil person at the same time."

Loved – Hashem loves emuna very much, as Rebbe Nachman writes (Sefer HaMidot, Emuna): "By virtue of emuna, a person is as beloved to Hashem as a wife is to her husband."

Delightful – Emuna is the delight of Hashem (See Likutei Moharan, I:97). Hashem adorns Himself with and delights in the emuna of the righteous, and loves to see what they accomplish with their prayers. Prayer is emuna. People with emuna are delightful to Hashem; the *tzaddikim* with steadfast emuna are Hashem's delight in creation.

Everything is For the Best

Now that we know that emuna is the world's most precious commodity, and that the entire purpose of Torah, mitzvot, and creation is to bring a person to emuna, we should know that the main principle of emuna is our faith that **everything is for the best**.

Any emuna that lacks the faith that everything is for the best is incomplete is accompanied by fantasies and disappointment. Emuna is synonymous with happiness and with prayer. One who claims to have emuna, but who is unhappy, and who fails to walk around with a song on his lips and with dancing feet that praise and thank Hashem, is contradicting himself. For one who truly believes that everything is for the best will always be singing, dancing, and happy. A person that only claims to have emuna, but who doesn't pray for all his needs, is again contradicting himself. If he had complete emuna, especially that Hashem is standing there right over his shoulder listening to every syllable of his prayers, he'd certainly pray at length and in great detail for all his needs.

In addition, we should know that the emuna that everything is for the best includes and encompasses all the aspects of emuna. One who believes that everything is for the best certainly believes in Divine providence, or *hashgacha pratit*. Everything is for the best because everything comes from Hashem as magnificent individually-tailored Divine providence. If anything in the world was left to chance, it would be impossible to declare that everything is for the best.

When we believe that everything is for the best, we certainly believe that everything that occurs in our lives has a message, a reason, and an ultimate purpose whose objective is to stimulate us to get closer to Hashem.

There is Nothing other than Him

In addition, when we believe that everything is for the best, we believe that there is no power in the world other than Hashem. One who believes that "there is nothing other than Hashem" never blames himself or others for anything, since everything comes from Hashem. As such, a person is spared from a long list of negative emotions such as anger, revenge, and frustration.

When we refrain from tormenting ourselves after a setback in life, we avoid depression, self-flagellation, and feelings of guilt, bitterness, and low self-esteem. When we don't blame others for our misfortunes, we don't fall into traps of hate, revenge, anger, and the like. By clinging to the belief that everything is for the best, we avoid every emotional difficulty in the world.

For example, with emuna, we avoid jealousy. King Solomon writes that jealousy causes the decay of one's bones - in other words, jealousy does serious damage to a person. Imagine a poor person who has emuna; he's not jealous of the rich person, for he believes that Hashem does everything for the best, and if he doesn't have much money, that's Hashem's will too. As such, he stays emotionally healthy, and avoids the pitfalls of jealousy and envy.

When we believe that everything is for the best, we're not constantly competing with other people, for we know that Hashem is leading us down our own special path for our own ultimate benefit - all according to our individual *tikkun* and task in life. With this in mind, we need not look enviously at anyone else, for each of us is doing his or her own prescribed mission on earth.

With emuna, we're never sad or disappointed. Even if someone is mean or unfair to us, we believe that everything comes from Hashem and that everything is for the very best. Rather than focusing on the person who's mistreating us, we focus on Hashem who is doing everything for our ultimate best.

We can conclude that the emuna that everything is for the best is the principle type of emuna that we should all pray for, since this emuna is a package deal of healthy emotions, favorable character, and salvations for all our problems. Although the road to emuna is not easy, knowing that this is the right road to take is already a major achievement. We should also strive to understand the value of what we're searching for: the entire redemption of our people as well as our own personal redemption depends on emuna.

Happy is the person that tenaciously searches for the lost princess – emuna – for he or she certainly brings untold gratification to the King, Hashem. Even when we don't see immediate results, we should be strong of heart. With desire and perseverance, each one of us will ultimately find our own lost princess, as Rebbe Nachman allegorically promised. With a strong will, each of us will attain complete emuna, which will hasten the spiritual rectification of the entire universe.

Chapter Three

Proper Personal Prayer

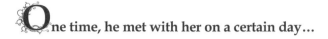

One time, he met with her on a certain day...

As we mentioned earlier, emuna itself is one of Hashem's creations. When the King meets with the princess, He meets with emuna. When any person meets with Hashem in seclusion – what we call *hitbodedut* or personal prayer – he or she connects with Hashem by way of emuna.

Correct Personal Prayer

Correct personal prayer is only possible once we approach Hashem with emuna, since this is an expression that we subjugate our own will to the will of Hashem. Whether or not Hashem answers our prayers, we're satisfied with Hashem's will. It doesn't matter to us whether Hashem says yes or no as we see in the following story (Kochavei Or, 77):

A man named Yisroel from the town of Nemirov begged Rebbe Nachman of Breslov to allow him to travel to a war zone for the purpose of making a living. Rebbe Nachman didn't want to agree under any circumstances, but he didn't want to take away Yisroel's free choice. Therefore, Rebbe Nachman advised him: "Imagine that you feel the same way whether you go or not, whether I say yes or no. Now, say five Psalms, and afterwards, do whatever comes to your mind." That's exactly what Yisroel did.

Later, he returned to Rebbe Nachman and said that "yes" came into his mind. Rebbe Nachman showed displeasure, for he knew that Yisroel's heart still leaned to the "yes", and was set on doing what he wanted to do. His lust for money was carrying him into grave danger...

According to the principles of emuna, we must know that only Hashem knows the designated path of an individual's particular mission on earth. When we believe this, a yes or no is the same to us; we're just as happy flying to New York as we are flying to Los Angeles, to make a living selling bagels or selling bonds, or to meet John Doe or Joe Crow. How? We know that everything Hashem is doing for us is for our ultimate best. When the "yes" and the "no" are the same to us, we gain an insight into what Hashem really wants from us. Hashem illuminates in our hearts exactly what we need to do.

The Baal Shem Tov once commented on the passage (Psalms 16:8), "I have set Hashem before me always," and asked, "How do I know that Hashem is before me always?" And he answered, "When I live a life of emuna, where everything is equal in my eyes, whether Hashem says 'yes' or 'no'."

To Do Your Will

In spirituality as well, when a person asks Hashem for whatever he or she needs to observe the Torah and to do Hashem's will, there is a prescribed path and pace of growth that only Hashem knows. So, even when we pray for spirituality, the "yes" and the "no" should be identical in our eyes. We shouldn't be disappointed when we don't get what we want. We should just continue praying.

Personal prayer with true emuna means that a person comes to Hashem and nullifies his or her own desires. Emuna is an aspect of *malchut*, and *malchut* has nothing other than what it receives from the six higher spheres. It's known in Jewish esoteric thought that when we nullify our ego, and we make Hashem's will our will, we attain royal virtues - such as patience - that are the result of emuna.

The core of proper *hitbodedut* is when a person searches for what Hashem wants from him or her. Here's an example: "Hashem, I have no idea what my true spiritual status is, or the proper path I need to take, or what to emphasize in my life, how I should pray, or even what I should pray for. But You know everything - where

I am in the world, what I should be doing, and how I should do it. Therefore, please have mercy on me, and give me the words that I need to speak to You today. Enable me to thank You for everything I need to thank You for, to evaluate myself properly, and to pray for whatever I need to pray for. Illuminate my heart with proper words of prayer..." and so forth.

Even when we know what we want to pray for, for example, if we've set aside a portion of our daily personal prayer to pray for improvement in a certain area, we should preface our prayer with the type of prayer in the previous paragraph, so that Hashem will direct us in the right path, give us the proper words, and enable us to pray at length.

With the type of *hitbodedut* that results from nullifying our own will, we never lose hope or patience. Indeed, when we walk the pleasant path of personal prayer with patience, Hashem opens our eyes and our mouths, so we can speak to Him properly. With proper personal prayer, Hashem most certainly sends us the proper things we need to say for our ultimate benefit and for the rectification of our souls, and we succeed in being the way Hashem wants us to be.

Chapter Four

Improper Personal Prayer

And he lost his temper at her, and an utterance escaped his mouth: "May the no-good-one take you!" In the evening she went to her room, and in the morning, no one knew where she was. Her father became very distraught, and he went everywhere looking for her.

Improper personal prayer angers the King. Improper personal prayer means that a person has lost emuna, in other words, his or her emuna has disappeared. This explains why Rebbe Nachman wrote (Sefer Hamidot, Anger): "Anger results from improper personal prayer," for Hashem's anger manifests itself within a person, and as soon as emuna disappears, a person becomes impatient and angry.

What Do You Really Want?

Improper personal prayer means that a person isn't searching for Hashem's will in his or her *hitbodedut*, but praying for his or her own desires and appetites, whether material or spiritual. That's not what Hashem wants; in effect, improper personal prayer is asking Hashem for help in doing the opposite of Hashem's will.

Proper personal prayer means that one nullifies one's own personal will in favor of Hashem's will, and that his or her entire *hitbodedut* revolves around this point – to nullify personal desires.

Improper personal prayer means that a person wants Hashem to nullify His will in favor of his or her own personal desires, and his or her entire *hitbodedut* revolves around this point – that Hashem should do that person's will.

Hashem doesn't like material requests for things that are needless in the service of Hashem. Spiritual requests are trickier: Sometimes, we fool ourselves into thinking that we're asking for spirituality, but our motives aren't always pure. We may think that we're asking for Torah scholarship, but deep down we want prestige, publicity, fame, and honor. We might want people to be kissing our hands, or whispering behind our back, "What a scholar! What a *tzaddik*! Look how holy he acts! He's the pillar of the universe..."

Even those of us that don't care about fame or prestige, but are serving Hashem in order to earn a lofty place in the world-to-come, are stilling missing the mark. Rebbe Nachman says (Likutei Moharan II:37), that just as some pursue their appetites in this world, others pursue their appetites in the next world. The latter is of course preferable, but still not the pure service of Hashem.

We can conclude that even in spirituality, we must nullify our desires in favor of Hashem's will, even when we're asking for spirituality. Many people fail to understand that their desires – even in spirituality – are none other than appetites and lusts, even though they're on a higher level than physical appetites and lusts. Spirituality seekers realize that bodily urges are nonsense, but they often make the mistake of substituting spiritual appetites such as wisdom, honor, rewards in the next world for bodily urges.

Let this be your guideline: The sign of improper personal prayer, when one asks Hashem to fulfill his or her desires, even spiritual desires that *seem* to be Hashem's will, is when a person feels angry afterward. When our desire is simply to serve Hashem, we never have sorrow or impatience if our prayers aren't answered, for we understand that Hashem wants us to continue to pray.

Bitul, or Nullification of Ego

When one engages in personal prayer without the objective of nullifying his or her own will in favor of Hashem's will, there is no way to achieve true proximity to Hashem. Such a person sees Hashem as a tool for fulfilling his or her own selfish desires – even spiritual ones. Needless to say, such *hitbodedut* irritates Hashem.

Rebbe Nachman teaches us the meaning of proper personal prayer (see Likutei Moharan I:52), when he teaches us that the main objective of *hitbodedut* is to reach a state of *bitul*, or nullification of ego, which enables a person to become one with Hashem. Any other intent in personal prayer other than *bitul* detracts from proper personal prayer.

Pursuing self-interests, without searching for what Hashem wants from us, is a sign of incomplete or blemished emuna. Blemished emuna arouses difficulties in life, stern judgments, and anger.

How does a person become ensnared in anger and impatience during personal prayer? The reason is simple – he or she is pursuing self-interests while ignoring what Hashem wants. These self-interests are so strong that a person could even be shaking a fist skyward when his or her demands aren't fulfilled. Needless to say, such anger and impatience are apostasy and a critical blow to emuna. Hashem decides how and when to answer prayers; any opposition to Hashem's will is therefore detrimental. So, when a person argues with Hashem, yells at Hashem (Heaven forbid!) and so forth, he or she falls into the trap of anger and severe judgments.

Every Moment in Hitbodedut

Know full well that *hitbodedut* should precede everything we do. Here's why: personal prayer enables us to collect our thoughts, to objectively evaluate ourselves, to compose ourselves, and to understand what Hashem wants us to do this very instant. As such, we can determine what the truth is, differentiate between right and wrong, decide what action to take and evaluate everything we do. We ask Hashem to guide us, to show us the right path, and to help us pursue it.

When we're undergoing a trying situation, and we compose ourselves in the proper manner, asking what Hashem wants from us and requesting His assistance, then we never transgress because our personal prayer has been proper. But, whenever someone makes an improper assessment, fails to ask what Hashem wants and doesn't pray to do Hashem's will, he or she transgresses and goes against Hashem's will. This is a result of improper personal prayer that arouses Hashem's displeasure.

In the morning, no one knew where she was...

As we mentioned earlier, the immediate outcome of Hashem's anger is that emuna disappears, and a person loses his or her connection with Hashem. A concerted effort is subsequently required to restore emuna.

Eve was the first person to make the mistake of improper personal prayer. She didn't compose herself to determine what was really true and therefore failed. She chose her own will – eating the forbidden fruit – instead of reminding herself of Hashem's will. The tragic result kindled Hashem's anger and caused a disappearance of emuna. Ever since, all of mankind has had to toil in order to find emuna.

Self-Composure

Here we arrive at one of the definitions of proper personal prayer – self composure. Rabbi Levi Yitzchak Binder of blessed memory – one of the last generation's prominent Breslover Chassidim – used "self composure" synonymously with *hitbodedut*. The most important aspect of self composure – stopping to think before we do or say something – is to determine the truth, so that it's crystal clear what Hashem wants from us in every single matter, thus dispelling all doubts. Self composure results in a strong conviction that never leaves us.

We have to believe in ourselves, namely, that our sincere personal prayer is leading us to truth, to the extent that no one or nothing can make us deviate from what we know is true. Furthermore, even if we have not yet achieved our objectives, and we know that the road to fulfilling our goal is long, difficult, and oftentimes challenging – we nonetheless continue steadfastly in the way that we know is truth. Knowing that our goal is truth, nothing in the universe should be able to weaken our resolve or to lead us astray. With such convictions, we will eventually succeed in realizing our goals to the extent that we no longer transgress; this is proper self composure.

As long as a person harbors the slightest doubt as to what truth or the proper course of action is, then the *Yetzer Hara*, or Evil Inclination, can easily tempt that person into making tragic mistakes. The Hebrew numerical equivalent for the word *saphek*, or doubt, is 240 – which is identical to the numerical equivalent of Amalek, who signifies the Evil Inclination. Our doubts are our Evil Inclination, which takes every opportunity to try to trip us, tempt us to transgress, and to damage our own souls Heaven forbid. By attempting to weaken us, the Evil Inclination attempts to prevent us from realizing our goals.

The fault of not knowing what is true is not only a fault in our belief in Hashem or in our belief in the great *tzaddikim*, **it's a fault in our belief in ourselves**. We have to believe in ourselves, namely, that whatever we learn from the Torah or hear from the *tzaddik* is absolute truth and the proper course of action. As such, we never surrender or compromise our convictions, we fight for the truth, and we certainly don't subjugate ourselves to anyone that leads us off that path. We must be strong and persistent to continue in the path of truth.

Believing in Ourselves

If we look at the Torah from beginning to end, we see that the failures and setbacks of our ancestors all stemmed from the fact that they didn't believe in themselves.

First, let's look at Eve, who was commanded not to eat from the Tree of Knowledge: When the serpent came to tempt her, he succeeded, because she didn't believe in herself. She wasn't 100% sure that what she heard from Adam her husband was the absolute truth, and the only truth, and that she must act accordingly.

With regard to Eve's transgression, our sages say: The teacher and the pupil – to whom do you listen? Hashem said not to eat from the tree – that's the teacher; the serpent said to eat from the tree – that's the pupil. So, to whom do you listen? Clearly, one should listen to the teacher; so why did Eve listen to the serpent?

Eve didn't believe in herself, that what she knew was the absolute, non-negotiable truth. Had she believed in herself, she wouldn't have been willing to listen to a single word from the serpent's mouth. She should have said, "This is truth, law, and totally binding! Mister Serpent, either change the subject, or take a walk! The Tree of Knowledge is off limits! Case closed!" Eve's failure to clarify the truth in her own mind was the very opening that allowed the serpent to lead her astray.

Adam, after hearing directly from the Creator that he may not eat from the Tree of Knowledge, also lacked belief in himself. Had the truth been clear in his mind, he would have been forceful and emphatic: "The fruit of the Tree of Knowledge is forbidden! This is the absolute truth that I clearly heard from the voice of Hashem! This is a non-negotiable fact!" If he had believed in himself, no power on earth could have swayed him, not even his wife Eve.

Here's another example – King Saul. He erred in that he didn't destroy the entire Amalekite nation as he was commanded, for he didn't believe in himself. As such, he let his people tempt him into sparing the Amalekite's flocks, and he himself refrained from killing the Amalekite king. Samuel the prophet chastised him (see Samuel I, chapter 15), and said, "If you consider yourself insignificant, remember that you are the head of the Tribes of Israel and Hashem anointed you as king over Israel!" In other words, Samuel's reprimand hones in on the fact that Saul didn't believe in himself and didn't believe in the fact that **Hashem** had anointed him as king, and that **he** should have decided what's proper in Hashem's eyes, and not the masses. Hashem commanded King Saul to wipe out the Amalekites and all their possessions, and specifically stipulated that not a single Amalekite animal be left alive. Had King Saul believed in himself, could anyone have swayed him?

And he Refused...

Let's look at an opposite example, of a *tzaddik* that had a firm belief in himself – Joseph. The truth was crystal clear in Joseph's mind, so when Potiphar's wife tried to tempt him, the Torah says, "And he refused." We sing this passage with the note that's called *shalshelet*, so when reading the Torah we draw out the word "refused" three times longer than most of the other notes that we use to chant the Torah reading. In essence, the Torah is telling us that Joseph refused, and refused, and refused! He had no doubt – another man's wife is forbidden! No insistence, goading, or temptation in the world could make Joseph veer from what he knew was the truth. He believed in himself: "This is what I learned! This is truth! This is how I must act!"

change direction   *urging on*

We also see at the end of Rebbe Nachman's Tale of the Lost Princess, that the viceroy attained such a strong measure of self composure that nothing could weaken his resolve. He never doubted what he believed was the truth, namely, that the princess had been taken to a mountain of gold and a castle of pearls, and that he must rescue her from there! Even when superhuman giants tried to convince him otherwise, and gave him strong evidence that there's no such thing as a mountain of gold and a castle of pearls, he remained unflinching in his resolve. As such, he ultimately succeeded in rescuing the princess.

forcible

Clarifying the Truth in its Entirety

This is the goal of *hitbodedut*, and only this is proper *hitbodedut*. In the first stage, we should clarify for ourselves point-by-point what the truth is according to our holy Torah and how we should act accordingly. We should know what Hashem wants from us in general and what the truth is in any particular instance. We must build a cogent and forceful measure of self composure: Such and such is the truth, and nothing in the world can make me deviate from it or give me the slightest shred of doubt. This is the meaning of believing in ourselves: we believe in every point that we've clarified for ourselves, and nothing can make us swerve from the truth.

+ turn aside

clear or plain

In the second stage, once we have clarified a certain point, and the truth is clear to us, we must now pray daily and ask Hashem to help us live according to this unequivocal point of truth, so that no one or nothing can make us deviate from the truth. We also have to ask Hashem to prevent our hearts from tempting us to act otherwise. Even after we've clarified the truth, we still have the long war against our internal enemy, the *Yetzer Hara*, or Evil Inclination, who incites the body against the soul. The *Yetzer* masterfully and cunningly incites a person to act in discordance with the truth, and makes a person forget the truth that he or she has already clarified. Avoiding the *Yetzer's* pitfalls requires daily and incessant prayer.

disputing — *never stopping*

Rebbe Nachman teaches (Rebbe Nachman's Discourses, 47): "Therefore, one must overcome and set aside the time required for composing oneself thoroughly, evaluating all one's actions in this world, whether it is befitting to spend one's days doing these particular actions. When a person doesn't compose himself, he doesn't know what he's doing, and even if he has an occasional measure of self composure, it doesn't last long, and his sense flees with the passing moments. Even the little sense he has isn't strong and forceful. For this reason, such people don't understand the folly of this world. But, if one had strong and forceful composure of the mind, he'd realize that everything is folly and nonsense..."

To Learn in Order to Do

Here's a practical example: A person learns that the Torah commands us to guard our eyes. This is an unequivocal commandment, anchored in Jewish religious law and elaborated in all the major works of ethics and Chassidic thought. Maybe he even heard lectures that aroused him, teaching that the only way to guard one's eyes is to close them. He also heard that one cannot attain this level without continual daily prayer, asking Hashem to help him fulfill the commandment of guarding his eyes.

With all this in mind, how can such a person walk down a city street with his eyes wide open, gazing in every direction? Simply, such a person lacks self composure, lacks proper personal prayer, and doesn't believe in himself! He has yet to clarify to himself that what he has learned is the absolute truth, and he hasn't prepared himself for a battle of no compromises – to judge himself every day on each and every forbidden sight, and to pray for help in guarding his eyes. Without concerted daily prayer for guarding one's eyes, it's impossible to avoid looking at forbidden sights.

Proper personal prayer means standing before Hashem with lengthy prayer, begging and requesting that we clarify this point of truth until no trace of doubt remains in our hearts: We must close our eyes to forbidden sights. There's no situation in the world that allows a person to look at a woman, other than members of one's immediate family. There's no mitzvah in the world that allows a person to look at a woman, other than choosing a wife. And there's no reason in the world for one to open one's eyes in a place where there are women.

Guard and Remember

As long as one sees that he continues to slip, he should persevere in prayer until he succeeds in guarding his eyes and no longer fails.

Once a person has achieved the ability of guarding his eyes, he needs continued daily prayer to maintain what he has worked so hard for. Only incessant daily efforts will assure guarding one's eyes completely, which means that one will be spared from uncountable transgressions, sins, and blemishes to his soul. By guarding one's eyes, one earns the title of a *tzaddik*, earns emuna, merits an abundance of income and miraculous Divine providence, gains a holy insight into Torah, and benefits from many more blessings.

Why lose all this? A person that doesn't believe in himself that the obligation of guarding one's eyes is absolute Torah truth won't fight to keep his eyes shut! If he'd believe in himself, he'd pray for this every day while clarifying the truth that looking at women is forbidden. He'd refuse to be tripped up in this area anymore. And if he did have a slip-up, he wouldn't ignore it. Instead, he would simply evaluate himself, make *teshuva*, and continue praying.

What is Transgression and Repeat?

Our sages say (tractate Yoma, 86), "Rav Huna said: Since a person transgressed and repeated the transgression, the forbidden deed becomes permissible in his mind." Something forbidden appears to be permissible unless we work hard daily to avoid it. As long as we keep up the fight, pray, evaluate ourselves, and make daily *teshuva*, then even a periodic slip-up is part of our growth, and clearly the transgression doesn't become permissible in our minds. If we make a mistake, we don't ignore it. On the contrary, we strengthen ourselves in *teshuva* and in prayer until we no longer transgress.

On the other hand, if one lacks proper personal prayer, and he hasn't clarified to himself that looking at women is forbidden, and it's not yet clear to him that as long as he continues to transgress he must add more prayer, more *teshuva*, and more hard work, and he doesn't work on his daily *hitbodedut*, then certainly the transgression will become permissible in his eyes. In other words, he won't feel that there's anything wrong with looking at women.

This is the true intent of our sages: Since a person transgresses and repeats the transgression, the forbidden deed becomes permissible in his mind – this is when there's no *teshuva* between each transgression. But, if a person slips up, does *teshuva* in the meanwhile, and then slips up again, the next time he transgresses is not called a repeat, because the act of *teshuva* erased the former transgression. This is one of the magnificent virtues of *hitbodedut*.

Even if a person doesn't succeed in observing what he knows is true, the important thing is that he *knows* what's true, fights for it, and evaluates himself daily. This is an enormous encouragement for those who pray and work on themselves, yet continue to fall from time to time. Rather than losing heart, they should regard their setback as part of their service to Hashem and their spiritual growth, and not as a failure.

We can apply everything we said about guarding our eyes to any mitzvah in the Torah, to improving any character trait, or to ridding ourselves of any bad habit or bodily lust. Whenever we take a certain issue and invest repeated personal prayer until we clarify the crystal-clear truth in our own mind, Hashem certainly helps us accomplish what we desire to accomplish. This is the path of righteousness, and of becoming a complete *tzaddik*.

Don't Go Away

Once Adam sinned, he caused a concealment of emuna; for that reason, every subsequent generation and every person must wage a big war to live according to emuna. Before man first sinned, emuna was crystal clear, and one could easily believe in Hashem. But since Adam made improper personal prayer, then an utterance escaped The King's mouth – Hashem – that the "no-good one should take you," and emuna, the princess, disappeared. Now, each of us has to work so hard to find emuna.

A person sins because he forgets Hashem, and turns his back on Hashem. Hashem responds in like manner, and turns His back on the sinner. Meanwhile, emuna becomes even more elusive. Each transgression that a person commits causes a deeper disappearance of emuna, making the search for emuna even more difficult. A person's entire task in the world should be to rectify the disappearance of emuna that he caused with his own actions.

On the other hand, we can take heart by knowing that if a person has sinned, and emuna is concealed, yet the person reinforces himself and strives to search for emuna, then not only will he rectify everything, but he will bring the world and himself to a higher level than if he had never sinned at all, as long as his transgression wasn't deliberate.

This is all the result of Hashem's mercy, for Hashem sees that a person doesn't willfully sin, yet his *Yetzer* overcomes and leads him astray. As such, Hashem gives us the gift of *teshuva*, and even rewards us by helping us turn our infamous past misdeeds into steppingstones of spiritual growth. Nevertheless, one should never willfully transgress in order to attain a *teshuva*-based *tikkun* afterwards. Our sages warned, "He who says, 'I shall sin and then make *teshuva*,' never has the chance to make *teshuva*."

The Ten Journeys of the Shechinah (Divine Presence)

The concept of emuna disappearing because of Hashem's anger is a recurring theme in the world, on both a general and a specific scale. In general, each time a generation's sins weigh heavier, emuna disappears even more. The Gemara in tractate Rosh Hashanah (page 31a) describes how the *Shechinah* left the Holy of Holies prior to the destruction of our Holy Temple in Jerusalem and says, "Rav Yehuda bar Idi says in the name of Rebbe Yochanan: The *Shechinah* traveled ten journeys - from the Ark of the Covenant to the cherub; from cherub to cherub; from cherub to the doorway; from the doorway to the courtyard; from the courtyard to the altar; from the altar to the roof; from the roof to the wall; from the wall to the city; from the city to the mountain; from the mountain to the desert; and from the desert, she ascended to sit in her place, for it is said, 'I shall return to My place (Hosea, ch. 5)'."

The meaning of this passage is that the more the Children of Israel sinned, the more the Divine Presence left them – step by step – until it disappeared totally and the Holy Temple was subsequently destroyed.

The Inner Wisdom of Prayer

The ramification of the *Shechinah*'s disappearance is the loss of emuna, as we see in the Arizal's explanation of the Holy Temple's destruction. Are we merely lamenting the destruction of wood and stones? Certainly not; the principle destruction is the destruction of emuna. The burning of the Holy Temple signifies the burning of prayer's inner wisdom, to the extent that man no longer feels the need to pray for his needs. The Holy Temple is called a "House of prayer for all nations," (see Isaiah, ch. 56).

The burning of the Holy Temple and the exile of the *Shechinah* mean that man lost the wisdom of emuna. We see this clearly, especially when a person has a problem or some type of trouble, and he or she thinks of every trick in the book or of every possible person that might offer advice or a solution rather than simply appealing to Hashem for help. The prayer that comes from true emuna has disappeared in exile because of our sins – this is the tragedy of the Holy Temple's destruction. Why? The emuna that leads to true and earnest prayer is the only true advice that one can depend on in any situation. Without it, a person is alone and helpless.

On an individual level, each time Hashem becomes angry, He hides Himself from a person. When Hashem hides His countenance from someone, emuna doesn't illuminate that person's soul and he or she finds praying difficult. Hashem is in effect saying: "Your life could be so pleasant with Me and you could have easily connected to Me. But because of your current unfortunate actions, your *tikkun* will be even more difficult, for you'll have to search for Me within the concealment that you caused. Now that you've sinned, you have to work much harder to find emuna." In reality, the only difficulty in the world is when emuna conceals itself from a person and darkness subsequently overcomes that person's soul.

From all this, one can now understand what happens when a person transgresses. The dark cloud of concealment that overcomes a person is the root of all troubles. The worst sins are those connected to lewdness, especially in light of Rebbe Nachman's teachings (see Likutei Moharan I:31) that the preservation of emuna depends on "guarding the covenant", simply speaking, personal holiness. Hashem conceals Himself from those who commit forbidden sexual acts, resulting in the transgressors' loss of emuna. Lost emuna is extremely difficult to restore.

We can now understand that the entire purpose of Torah and mitzvot are to find and restore our lost emuna. Moreover, if a person fails to learn Torah with the intent of attaining emuna and getting to know Hashem, then the Torah and mitzvot won't bring him closer to Hashem at all.

There's No Punishment in the World at All

Ever since the time of Adam and Eve, whenever one sins, the darkness of concealment becomes stronger. Each blemish causes additional concealment of Hashem's illumination - emuna. The more Hashem is concealed, the harder it is to find emuna. Hashem says explicitly in the chastisements of *Parshat Ki Tavo* (see Devarim, ch. 31), "I shall hide My countenance on the day because of the evil." Rebbe Nachman alludes to this in our tale at hand, for each time the viceroy doesn't do what he's supposed to, then the princess goes further away, requiring much more effort to find her.

In reality, there is no punishment in the world; the blemish of a misdeed is itself the punishment. King David writes (Psalms 34:22), "the death blow of the wicked is evil." Obviously, drinking poison is dangerous; the subsequent poisoning is not a punishment but an outcome. Therefore, the fool who drinks poison has no one to blame but himself. Likewise, one who sins forfeits Hashem's illumination suffers from concealment. The concealment is not a vindictive punishment from Hashem, but the result of the sinners own misdeed. Therefore, there's no room for the sinner to complain to Hashem about his misfortunes, for they are the outcome of his own actions.

The way to rectify the downward spiral of sin and concealment is to declare a new beginning, which means one should compose oneself and strive for proper personal prayer that seeks to answer the question, "What does Hashem want from me, now that I have sinned?" Imagine a dialog with Hashem like this: "Shall I fall into depression and despair? Of course, not! That's certainly not what You want from me, Hashem! I know, I should strengthen myself from this moment on to believe in You, that You are everywhere, and from this very moment, I'll do my best to find You and to get close to You. I want to be a better person, Hashem!" If a person speaks to Hashem in this way, his or her spiritual nosedive will become a jet-propelled takeoff and failure will become success.

There's No Sadness in the World at All

The sorrow and misfortune that a person has in life is the result of concealment. Why? If a person wouldn't sin, he or she wouldn't lose Hashem's illumination and suffer the subsequent concealment which manifests itself as darkness in their souls. Where there's no concealment, there's no sorrow and misfortune. As long as one retains the light of emuna – which as we explained is Hashem's illumination of the soul and the opposite of concealment and darkness – one doesn't feel any sorrow or deficiency. Rebbe Nachman teaches (Likutei Moharan I:250), that a person feels sorrow as a result of deficient spiritual awareness, namely, that he or she lacks the emuna that everything in the world comes from Hashem and that everything is for the very best.

Describing the hardship of Israel as slaves in Egypt, the Torah says (Shemot 6:9), "But they did not listen to Moses because of impatience and hard work." Rebbe Nachman interprets "impatience" as a deficiency of emuna, to teach that the main suffering of the Israelites as slaves was their deficiency of emuna. Conversely, Rebbe Nachman cites "patience" as indicative of emuna (see Likutei Moharan I:155). We therefore learn a pattern of cause-and-effect in the suffering of Israel in Egypt, as the deficiency of emuna, or "impatience," led to "hard work" - a life of toil and trouble.

The Israelites as slaves in Egypt didn't believe in Divine providence. This was their sorrow that led them to complain and to fall into depression. They were so deeply despaired that not even the message of redemption brought them joy, for they didn't believe in it. When a person falls from emuna, his or her thought process and powers of reason are sorely constricted. Such a person isn't even able to absorb a good word or good tidings.

We Remembered the Fish... and the Squash...

Harsh external conditions were not *the* bitter factor in the Israelites' suffering in Egypt. Let's examine for a moment the notion of hard work; is this alone a reason for despair? Many people work extremely hard from sunup until sundown, and yet they're neither sad nor depressed. If the Children of Israel would have had complete emuna, that Hashem wanted them to toil as construction laborers for their ultimate benefit – both individual and collective – they'd have toiled willingly with no sorrow. One's torture and bitterness in life is certainly the outcome of a lack of emuna – failing to recognize that everything is the result of Hashem's precise Divine providence and all for the best. Without emuna, one cannot fully cope with a difficult situation.

The Torah provides additional evidence that Israel's suffering was not the result of slavery and forced labor: After Israel was freed from bondage, they didn't work at all. They ate the manna – the bread from Heaven – and were at leisure all day long to learn Torah and to get close to Hashem. Yet they still complained, and even expressed longing for Egypt! "The people became complainers... 'We remember the fish that we ate in Egypt... the squash and the watermelon...'" (Bamidbar 11: 1-6). What happened all of a sudden? Amnesia? Did they forget about the back-breaking work in the hot sun? \ *loss of memory*

From this passage we learn that the lack of emuna embittered Israel much more than slavery and hard work. As long as the Children of Israel lacked emuna, even after their redemption from bondage, they remained embittered. No matter what Hashem and Moses did for them, they complained. Even when Hashem was about to give them the most precious land on earth – the Land of Israel – they complained. What did they complain about? They were suspicious of a land that is capable of flowing with milk and honey, or whose fruit are oversized and too sweet. "Hey, something's wrong here...," they said to each other. Without emuna, a person complains about everything, including the best gifts in life.

As such, there is no reality of "bad"; one's outlook on a scale from good to bad depends on the level of one's emuna. The more the emuna, the happier and the more optimistic a person is. Unfortunately, the opposite is also true. Without emuna, life seems bad and pessimistic. Emuna – or the lack of it - determines a person's mood and state of mind much more than external influences and circumstances.

The practical expression of emuna is when we're satisfied with our lot in life. It doesn't matter where we are or what we're doing. When we believe that our present circumstance is the fruit of Hashem's infinite Divine and personal providence and all for the best, we're happy in whatever we're doing, *despite the hardships*. Without emuna, a person isn't happy even in a grand mansion with lush gardens, servants, swimming pool, tennis courts, two Lamborghinis and an unlimited bank account. Many are the rich and famous who lived (and still live!) lives of deep depression.

To Want what Hashem Wants

This explanation can also serve as an explanation for the entire Torah, namely, that transgression results from a lack of emuna. Every sin led to a free-fall into the darkness of concealment that necessitates even more effort in finding the lost emuna. This is a template for people's setbacks and failures since the beginning of time.

Therefore, if you feel that you're in a state of darkness, and emuna seems to be light years away, don't lose heart! Just like the viceroy, as soon we renew the search for emuna – and never give up – this in itself rectifies the blemish of our misdeeds that caused the disappearance of emuna. Hashem wants us to strive for emuna, and we should want what Hashem wants. When we do, each of us will succeed in finding his or her own individual princess while correcting all the blemishes of our past, and everything will fall into place. With emuna, there's always a happy ending.

Chapter Five

A Father's Mercy

Her father became very distraught, and he went everywhere looking for her

Even though Hashem sees that He has no choice but to conceal His Divine light from a person, He is extremely sorry, for the prophet says (Isaiah 63:9), "In their troubles, He is troubled." "Their troubles" alludes to the concealment of Divine illumination, for as we learned in the previous chapter, this is the source of all trouble. But, as long as a person remains steadfast and clings to emuna – which in and of itself is Hashem's illumination – then he or she is not in trouble even in the most trying situation. With emuna, not only do we spare ourselves loads of trouble and sorrow, but we also spare our merciful Father in Heaven the sorrow He feels for a person in sorrow.

Hashem wants to lavish His magnificent illumination on each of us, as a loving father desires to give to his beloved child. Yet, our misdeeds cause concealment. When a person falls into the darkness of concealment, Hashem is deeply sorry and prays for that person. The Gemara in tractate Berachot, page 7a, teaches us that Hashem Himself prays, for Hashem says: "'I shall bring them to My holy mountain and I shall gladden them in My house of prayer' – *My* house of prayer not *their* house of prayer, to teach that Hashem prays. And what does Hashem pray? Mar Zutra bar Tuvia says in the name of Rav: May it be My will that My mercy overcomes My wrath, and may mercy permeate all of My traits, and may I act with My children with the measure of mercy, and may I judge them with lenience."

"I shall gladden them in My house of prayer," is also alluding to the fact that Hashem gives each of us a personal redemption, making us happy by bringing us to emuna and to prayer, Because redemption and happiness are the result of emuna. As such, "I shall gladden them," by bringing them happiness and illuminating their souls by bringing them to "My house of prayer" - teaching them emuna and prayer. Dear reader, this is happening to you this very minute, for this book in your hands is a clear sign that Hashem is bringing you to emuna. What could be more gratifying to know?

Mitigating the Wrath and Revealing the Concealment

Let's analyze Hashem's prayer to Himself, as mentioned in the passage above: "May it be My will that My mercy overcomes My wrath..." is none other than Hashem's prayer that the concealment of His Divine Countenance be revealed, for His wrath in itself is concealment. This concept is easily understood with the following example: Imagine that your friend is upset with you. You know that now is not the time to ask favors from him or her, for clearly, he or she doesn't want to hear from you at all. You sense the ill-feeling, and you don't even consider the idea of requesting anything at this time from your friend. By the same token, when Hashem is angry at someone, that person is virtually unable to pray.

At this point, any of us would be shocked: "This is scary! What do I do if Hashem is angry at me, and I open my mouth to pray and nothing comes out? How can I live for a day like this with no prayer?"

Rebbe Nachman of Breslov says that there's no reason for despair - ever. The moment a person begins to make *teshuva* on his or her loss of emuna, and this very minute decides to search for emuna, Hashem's wrath is mitigated. The person's loss of emuna triggered Hashem's wrath in the first place, so his or her opposite action – the search and yearning to return the emuna – arouses unlimited Divine mercy, mitigating all severe judgments and turning them into mercy. Mercy is a Divine illumination; when Hashem illuminates our souls, it's so much easier to acquire emuna. If we continue with this example, when our angry friend is placated and forgiving, it's so much easier to request something from him or her. Now, we can fully understand the nature of Hashem's prayer to Himself, that His mercy may overcome His wrath, in order to prevent the concealment of His Divine illumination.

The Most Beautiful Revelation

When all is said and done, everything is for the very best! Concealment is a *tikkun*, or rectification in and of itself, for it stimulates a person to build, yearn and toil for new *kelim*, or spiritual vessels, which will enable us to absorb Divine illumination. Our *ratzon* - the will, efforts, and yearning to seek Hashem - is a prime vessel for the Divine illumination of emuna just as a crystal goblet is for a fine wine. We wouldn't want to pour a thirty year-old Chateau de Rothschild Cabernet wine in a broken or dirty glass, for the wine would either spill on the floor or become ruined. A fine wine necessitates a whole and immaculately clean goblet. By the same token, without proper vessels, a person can't receive Divine illumination. Hashem doesn't want to spill His "fine wine" on the floor – we must be able to contain it.

Without challenges and times of difficulty in our lives, we'd never seek emuna. If someone had perfect health, plenty of money, career success, marital bliss, and wonderful children, he or she would most likely never seek Hashem. Hashem doesn't want a person to stagnate spiritually. In that respect, concealment is a gift. The life difficulties that are manifestations of concealment stimulate prayer. Deficiency ignites effort and yearning to seek Hashem. Effort and yearning in turn build new and stronger vessels to hold the Divine illumination of emuna that brings us closer to Hashem.

Breslover tradition, handed down from teacher to pupil for the last two hundred years, teaches that in the future – after the sin of Adam is rectified – the world will be far more beautiful than it would have been had Adam never sinned.

With the aggregate of the entire world's prayers and upheavals resulting from concealment throughout the generations, and all the world's efforts to reveal the concealment since the dawn of mankind, imagine what beautiful new and wonderful vessels we now have, that were nonexistent before Adam sinned. These vessels will hold the illumination that reveals an exquisitely beautiful and rectified world that's beyond our wildest dreams.

Once Adam sinned, when good and evil became mixed, the world was in need of a *tikkun*; this *tikkun* requires prayer. Prayer has the power of converting extreme unholiness into a vessel of holiness.

I Cried Out from the Depths

A setback in life is really beneficial, as long as a person doesn't lose heart from it. If a setback stimulates a new beginning and a better second effort, it's wonderful! Rebbe Nachman cites Jonah's cry from deep inside the belly of the whale (see Rebbe Nachman's Discourses, 302) as the type of prayer we should all strive for. Only the earnest cries of a broken heart can pierce all barriers, and uplift the world from the depths of impurity.

Rather than losing heart from the setback, one needs to arouse oneself and earnestly seek to reveal the concealed emuna, which makes the person – and the world – much more beautiful than if the emuna were never concealed at all. A setback and its subsequent yearning and renewed effort bring out the best in a person. Life's extreme difficulties reveal such lofty traits as valor and dedication, which make a person and the world so much more beautiful.

In truth, nothing is more beautiful than the pure prayer of a poor person that flows forth from a broken heart. That's why Rebbe Menachem Mendel of Kotsk would always say, "**Nothing is more whole than a broken heart!**"

The viceroy stood up, for he saw that the king was very troubled, and asked that he provide him with a servant, a horse, and money for the journey, and set out to search for her...

Seeing the king's distress, the viceroy set out to search for the lost princess. This task – the search for emuna, to reveal the concealment of Divine illumination, to discover that Hashem is the King, that there's a Creator who governs the world with a mind-boggling precision down to the tiniest detail, and that everything He does is for the very best – is the task of every one of us. Certainly, the great *tzaddikim* are more preoccupied with this task than the man on the street, and on a higher level than the average person, but that doesn't prevent or exempt each of us from doing our part. Each of us must reveal his or her own private princess, his or her personal portion of emuna, and thereby contribute to the rectification of the entire world until everyone recognizes the Monarchy of Hashem.

For Hashem's Sake

When asking for emuna, one needs a pure motive and not personal interest or gain. As we see in our tale at hand, the king's distress motivated the viceroy to set out on the search, not the latter's hope of reward and the like. We too should seek emuna simply for Hashem's sake, for that's what Hashem wants from us, and not for any other reason such as eternal bliss or the title of "*tzaddik*" and so forth - and certainly not for material reasons such as enhanced income and good health.

Why? Hashem created the world for a purpose. He desires that we feel sorry when His will is not fulfilled in the world, and the world fails to fulfill its obligations to Hashem.

The purpose of the world is to reveal Hashem's monarchy, so that every living thing shall know that Hashem is the King, as we pray on Rosh Hashanah: "And every creature shall know that Hashem created it, and every living thing shall declare, Hashem the God of Israel is King, and His dominion is over everything." This is emuna.

A servant, a horse, and money for the journey...

The viceroy requested three tools to help him perform his task in the world. The servant is allegorical to the soul, the horse symbolizes the body, and money for the journey represents a livelihood.

The viceroy only requested money for the journey to perform his task. We too need an income in order to live in this world and to do our task of searching for emuna. Yet, the tool of an income should not be confused with the task at hand. One should not devote an entire life to searching for more money – the tool – rather than searching for emuna – the task. When a person first sets out on the search for emuna, he or she doesn't yet have a strong spiritual vessel of trust in Hashem. Therefore, one is advised to ask Hashem for an income as a free gift, since he or she doesn't yet have the proper level of trust in Hashem that justifies the abundance of an adequate income. We all need enough to live on so that we can serve Hashem with composure, until we attain the proper level of trust in Hashem. As we see in our tale, the viceroy attained a befitting level of trust only in the end after extensive toil. Until then, his income was a free gift.

Until I Become a Kosher Person

We learn this concept from Rebbe Nathan of Breslov: When he first became a disciple of our holy Rebbe Nachman, he had terrible distress from his wife, his parents, and his in-laws. Their main complaint was, "How will you make a living if you're learning and praying all day long?" Rebbe Nathan gave in, and opened a store. His wife waited on customers, but she didn't know the prices of the goods, so she had to run back and forth between the store and the study hall to ask Rebbe Nathan. Clearly, that's not the way to run a business, and they suffered with a meager income. In his sorrow, Rebbe Nathan prayed to Hashem like this:

"Hashem! For one to deserve money without toil, one must be a kosher person. Until I become a kosher person, it'll take time. In the meantime, please give me an income as a free gift, so that I can serve You and rectify myself and become a truly kosher person."

Hashem heeded Rebbe Nathan's prayer, the product of a broken heart. At the same time that Rebbe Nathan prayed, his father met with his business partners, who came up with a superb idea: "Since your son Nathan yearns to spend each waking hour in the service of Hashem and learning Torah, and his mind isn't into commerce, give us his inventory and we'll buy and sell for him. We'll send him his periodic share of the profits, so he won't have to leave the house of study anymore."

Rebbe Nathan's father agreed, and from that day on Rebbe Nathan received his monthly profits without lifting a finger in commerce. His one prayer – the prayer of a broken heart – opened up the gate of abundance for many years.

As such, the viceroy is in essence asking from Hashem a livelihood as a free gift, so that he can embark on his journey to seek emuna.

And set out to ask for her...

We must note Rebbe Nachman's choice of terms; he tells us that the viceroy set out to "ask" for the lost princess, rather than "search" for her. Rebbe Nachman is telling us that one doesn't have to search for emuna, for emuna is right here, but concealed. Our job is to *ask* for emuna, constantly yearning, praying, and appealing to Hashem's Divine mercy until the concealment ends and emuna is revealed to us.

He asked exhaustingly for a very long time, until he found her. (And following is the account of how he asked for her, until he found her). He went from place to place, for a very long time, in deserts, fields and forests. And he asked for her a very long time.

Rebbe Nachman emphasizes the efforts of the viceroy, telling us that "**He asked exhaustingly for a very long time**." This shows the enormous desire that's required in order to find the lost princess. Rebbe Nachman is teaching us that we should seek, ask, and desire emuna with our hearts and all our might, with all our senses and with all our desires. And despite our efforts and our yearning, we should still know that it will take time until we find the lost princess.

scatter

One must carefully prepare for a long journey. Likewise, we too must make the proper emotional preparation – equipping ourselves with the needed patience, personal commitment, and desire that our journey will require. Seeking emuna is likely to be a long and difficult process, strewn with obstacles of every shape and form, and sometimes frustrating and disappointing. But, we should never surrender our desires and never submit to despair. With perseverance – as Rebbe Nachman teaches us – each of us will ultimately find his or her own lost princess.

Chapter Six

A Path to the Side

As he was crossing a desert, he saw a path to the side, and he was composing himself: "Seeing that I've been going such a long time in the desert and I cannot find her, I'll try this path - maybe I'll come to a settled area..."

After years of asking for the lost princess, the viceroy suddenly sees a path to the side. He decides to depart from the beaten track in favor of pursuing this path to the side. This is allegorical to the discovery of a new type of prayer – the personal prayer, or *hitbodedut*, which takes us off the beaten track of prayer that most people pursue.

A "path" is a narrow way with room for single-file walking only. As such, "path" signifies personal prayer.

Even though we have many exalted and wonderful prescribed prayer collections such as our prayer books, Psalms, *Likutei Tefillot*, and more, to find the lost princess - emuna - we need personal prayer.

Now we can understand what the viceroy seems to be saying to himself: "I've been walking down the beaten path for years, and I haven't yet found the lost princess..." – he's been on the same beaten track that everyone else uses, the well-known road of prescribed prayer. This is a road that never changes and that everyone knows. This is allegorical to one's rote daily praying, which hasn't been enough for finding emuna. But suddenly, the viceroy sees a path to the side, and composes himself: "I'll try this path! Maybe it will lead me to a settled area!" **Sure enough, when he took this path, he found the princess**.

The viceroy understood that he must connect his personal prayer – his soul-searching, praises and thanks to Hashem, reflections, and requests that reflect his individual soul's daily and hourly needs – to his unique situation at any given time. This is a prayer than cannot be written or prescribed anywhere, for it changes from moment to moment like a kaleidoscope, whose exquisite colors reflect the time, place, and individual circumstance of the body and soul. The viceroy realized that only this type of prayer can take him to a "settled area", a place where he can settle the turmoil within his soil and attain his true *tikkun*, or soul correction.

Every Morning is New

Each of us has his or her own individual personal path. Our path in life is as unique as our fingerprint, in accordance with our mission in life, former reincarnations, and our individual *tikkun*. Although there are general tasks that each person must do on this earth, each person has a unique and individual way of completing a given task. One cannot attain happiness or fulfillment in life without ascertaining his or her unique path. Without personal prayer, this is virtually impossible. Personal prayer can't be found in any book; not only does it change from person to person, it changes within a person himself from day to day and from hour to hour, according to a person's current circumstances and according to the stimuli that Hashem sends at that given moment.

We can therefore conclude that personal prayer varies from day to day. Yesterday's prayers don't necessarily answer today's needs. Every single day, each of us must ask: "What does Hashem want from me today – here and now? What must I correct, what must I pray for, how should I thank Hashem for the past and request my needs for the future?" Each morning is new. Each day has special things to thank Hashem for. The way and depth of expressing our gratitude to Hashem vary according to a person's spiritual cognizance at any given time and according to his or her current circumstance. *awareness*

The two most important elements of personal prayer, as we mentioned earlier, are **clarifying the truth** and **composing ourselves**. With self composure, we literally expand our powers of mind and soul. The search for truth keeps those powers on the right track. As in navigation, maintaining the proper heading assures a safe arrival at our destination.

The Point of Truth within the Truth

Proper personal prayer requires a point of truth. For example, when we seek a solution to - or salvation from - a problem or deficiency, we must first pray for emuna. That way, we can believe that all of life's difficulties come from Hashem and are His will. We should know that Hashem does nothing at random, and that everything is precisely directed from above.

Afterwards, we should ask Hashem to help us believe that everything is for the very best – even the problems and deficiencies – in order to help us accomplish our mission in life. True, we all want to solve our problems quickly. But, the point of truth within the truth is that our problems are a personal message from Hashem, to facilitate our soul correction and the performance of our mission on earth. Therefore, we should ask Hashem to instill in us the desire to comprehend the underlying message of our problem, deficiency, or tribulation, rather than the desire to be rescued from it.

equivalent

The point of truth within the truth of personal prayer is the desire to establish a connection with Hashem and to understand His messages. Complaints about those messages – which often manifest themselves as trials and tribulations – are tantamount to telling Hashem that one doesn't want to listen to Him, Heaven forbid. "Go away, Hashem! I don't want to listen to what You're trying to tell me..." is the statement of the complainer. If getting closer to Hashem is truth, then distancing oneself from Hashem is the opposite.

The complainer forgets the important point; namely, that all his troubles are gifts from Hashem to bring him closer. Every trial and tribulation carries its own message. Hashem never punishes – He educates and communicates. If a person's sole desire is to get rid of the trial or tribulation, then how will he learn what Hashem wants him to learn? What about all the enhanced tools – intellect, experience, and abilities - that Hashem wants to give by way of the trials and tribulations?

Hashem sends a myriad of messages to us every day. Some are designed to stimulate *teshuva* for a particular misdeed. Some are designed to lead a person to the performance of a given mitzvah. Still others are aimed at arousing us from our spiritual slumber so that we won't stagnate. *dull or sluggish*

So long as a person desires a quick solution to a problem, he or she won't avoid a negative attitude toward Hashem. King Solomon said (Proverbs 13:12), "A drawn out hope brings sickness to the heart." Simply hoping for a solution doesn't solve a problem, and only brings a person to complain that Hashem isn't answering his or her prayers. But, once a person understands Hashem's message that's concealed within the problem, then Hashem doesn't need the problem anymore.

The Point of Truth at all Costs

Even if are not yet living the point of truth within the truth, and we're not capable of personal prayer that's directed at getting to know Hashem rather than at quick solutions either, we should still never surrender the point of truth, which is: *"There is no one other than Hashem. I am null. There is no address for anything other than Hashem. Only Hashem can help me. Only Hashem knows what's best for me. I have no idea what my soul came down to this earth for and what the challenges are that I must face. Only Hashem knows."*

When we truly evaluate ourselves, and realize how difficult it is to know what Hashem truly wants from us in our particular circumstance, then we should appeal to Hashem with this point of truth, and beg Him, asking: *"Hashem, please have mercy on me. Teach me how to do Your will! I have no idea where I am in the world or where I should be going. Should I pray for a certain thing that's not what I have in mind? What points in my character should I be working on? Where should I be more elaborate or specific in my prayers? Hashem, please direct me! Only You can lead me down the right path for me!"*

This way, anyone can arrive at the type of earnest personal prayer that opens Heavenly doors. Such prayers – the prayers of a poor person in the doorway – are especially beautiful and unlock the true gates of salvation.

> **A** nd he went a very long time on that path. **Afterward, he saw a castle, with several soldiers standing guard around it. The castle was very attractive, well-built, and extremely orderly with the guards Posted...**

The viceroy reached an extremely beautiful castle, about which he knew nothing...

> **...and he was worried that the guards would not let him in. But he composed himself and said, "I will go and try..."**

The viceroy saw the castle surrounded by walls and guards, rendering any logical chance of entering impossible. But, he stopped and composed himself, coming to the superb conclusion that he'll go and try anyway. Likewise, a person that's faced with difficulties in life shouldn't be discouraged by the "high walls," the apparent obstacles that stand in the way. Personal courage means trying anyway, for without trying, there's certainly no success. So, if we try, what do we have to lose?

Rebbe Nachman of Breslov addresses this issue (see Likutei Moharan I: 115), saying:

"'And the people stood from afar, and Moses approached the thick cloud where God was, (Shemot 20:18).' One who walks the path of materialism his whole life, and then becomes enthused and desires to walk in the ways of Hashem, then the [Hashem's] Measure of Judgment accuses that person, and prevents him from walking in the ways of Hashem, and summons an obstacle where Hashem Himself is concealed within that obstacle.

"A man of reason, when examining the obstacle, finds Hashem... a man without reason sees an obstacle and immediately retreats.

"An obstacle is an aspect of the thick cloud. The thick cloud is darkness. 'And the people stood from afar,' for the masses retreat when they see an obstacle. But Moses, the epitome of reason and spiritual cognizance, 'approached the thick cloud where God was,' in other words, Moses approached the obstacle, for he knew that Hashem was hiding within the cloud."

Rebbe Nachman is teaching us that the incognizant fall into despair the moment they see an obstacle. Even if such a person does try to overcome, he quickly gives up and says, "This isn't for me!" But a person with sense - with even a minimal measure of spiritual cognizance - isn't incapacitated by the mere thought of an obstacle, for he knows that Hashem is everywhere, within the obstacle too! Such a person composes himself and says, "I'll give it a try! What do I have to lose? If Hashem wants me to succeed, I'll succeed! And if I don't succeed, my lack of success is also a message from Hashem, so I'll try and understand the message."

So he left the horse behind, and approached the castle. And the guards ignored him and did not hinder him. He went from room to room without disturbance, and came to one reception hall, where the king sat, wearing his crown. And there were a number of guards, and musicians with their instruments standing before him. It was all very pleasant and beautiful, and neither the king nor any of the others asked him anything at all...

When the viceroy makes an innocent effort to enter the castle, it turns out that no one is standing in his way, neither guards nor anyone else. He enters, and roams freely until he reaches the hall of the king.

The reason that no one hinders the viceroy is that he **prayed extensively**. When a person invests effort in prayer, then he benefits from Divine assistance in accomplishing his task. Even the *Yetzer Hara* helps a person that prays, for it is written (see Proverbs, ch. 16), "When Hashem is pleased with a person's ways, even his enemies will reconcile with him."

It turns out that a person with true emuna doesn't have an Evil Inclination at all, for he sees Hashem in everything, even in the difficulties that one normally attributes to the Evil Inclination himself. A person with emuna knows that even the *Yetzer Hara* is in Hashem's hands, and all the *Yetzer's* obstacles and temptations are the products of Divine providence. The apparent hindrances in our life are all from Hashem for our ultimate welfare, so that we'll seek Hashem, intensify our prayers, and search for Hashem's wisdom in every little thing until we attain the level of perfect emuna.

A person that lives a life of emuna is exclusively tied to Hashem; such a person never rubs elbows with the Evil Inclination at all. When he encounters an obstacle, he knows that the obstacle is from Hashem and all for the best. He's neither weakened nor scared away. He doesn't become confused and disoriented – he just increases his prayers and his requests for Hashem's help. As such, he serves Hashem with all his faculties – with his Good Inclination and his Evil Inclination alike.

Anytime that a person walks in the path of emuna and prays profusely for whatever he needs, then everyone comes to his aid, even the *Sitra Achra* (dark side) and the *Yetzer Hara* themselves. Even the forces of evil are subservient to Hashem, and as soon as Hashem decides that a person deserves something, then everyone must implement the Divine decision and assist the person whom Hashem favors. As such, things fall into place without hindrances.

Rebbe Nathan of Breslov said before his death: "During my old age everything is falling into place because I spent so much time in personal prayer during my younger years."

And he saw there delicacies and fine foods, and he stood and ate and went to lie down in a corner, to see what would transpire there...

besides

"He stood" means that he prayed, for standing (in Hebrew, *amida*) connotes prayer. We see here – as in the continuation of our tale – that the viceroy doesn't do a thing without praying beforehand; he therefore prays before he eats, and then lies down in a corner.

The viceroy lies down in the corner for three particular reasons:

make known

1. Common sense and personal safety. He doesn't yet know anything about where he is. Therefore, he doesn't want to be noticed and to attract attention. Who knows who these people are – good or evil? Maybe it's harmful to speak to them, to divulge information, or to come under their influence? Because of these uncertainties, he preferred "to lie down in a corner," in other words, to be inconspicuous.

2. Propriety. A new person in a new place should strive to blend in with the new surroundings rather than clamor for attention. It's best to refrain from forcing oneself on others, bothering them, or trying to become involved in other people's affairs. No one likes a loud and gaudy nuisance, especially if the nuisance is a new person in a new place.

3. Modesty. The prophet Micah said, "Walk modestly with your God." A servant of Hashem should always try to be quiet and modest, speaking only when necessary, and not searching for fame and glory. As such, the viceroy preferred to remain on the side, in the shadows…

followed

He saw that the king summoned for the queen. They went to bring her, and there ensued a great commotion and joy. The musicians played and sang a great deal, in that they were bringing the queen. They placed a chair for her and sat her next to the king. And she was the above-mentioned princess, and he (the viceroy) saw and recognized her. After that, the queen gazed about and saw a man lying in a corner, and recognized him. She stood from her chair and went over to him,

nudging him, and asked him, "Do you recognize me?" He answered, "Yes, I do. You're the lost princess." And he asked her, "How did you get here?" She answered, "Because my father blurted out the words `The no good one should take you', and here, this place, is no good..."

The viceroy finds the princess is in a place of evil - that of the *Sitra Achra*, the dark side. It turns out that the dark side also has a king – an old and foolish one, with servants, guards, noblemen, and all the equivalent hierarchy and counterparts of the holy side. Even the foolish old king of evil knows that emuna is the most important thing in the world, so he has captured the princess – emuna – and is keeping her captive in his domain.

This is the war of the dark side – to take away a person's emuna. Our job is to redeem our emuna from the dark side's impure hands and cling tightly to her, never losing her again.

A nd he asked her, "How did you get here?" **She answered, "Because my father blurted out the words `The no good one should take you', and here, this place, is no good..."**

We also learn from here just how cautious a person should be before uttering a spoken word. The consequences of a negative utterance are liable to be far-reaching and tragic, as we see here in our tale: The king's one utterance led to a terrible outcome, that his daughter the princess would fall captive in the castle of the evil *Sitra Achra*, the "no good one."

~ descriptive expression

Negative speech includes any undesirable remark in addition to epithets or insults. Bad tidings, unfavorable predictions, or finding fault with both people and things are liable to cause serious damage. Good speech, on the other hand, is beneficial to us and to our surroundings.

Chapter Seven

There is No Concealment

So he told her that her father is very sorry, and has been searching for several years...

One must know that the disappearance of emuna within a person is Hashem's greatest sorrow. Even if a person is suffering from a temporary setback in Torah learning, experiencing difficulty in performing a certain mitzvah, or fighting what seems to be a losing battle with a bad habit or bodily urge, as long as he or she clings to the emuna that everything is for the best – and continues to talk to Hashem about all these difficulties – Hashem doesn't have sorrow from that person.

But, when someone has trials, tribulations, and setbacks while disregarding Hashem and blames the whole world for his or her troubles, then Hashem is much more disturbed by the absence of that person's emuna than by his or her difficulties and failures.

Whatever happens to a person must happen; the test is whether that person will cling to the emuna that everything is from Hashem and for the very best. Indeed, Hashem's entire desire in creating the world is that people believe in Him, speak to Him, ask Him for all their needs, and learn that everything He does is for the very best. The objective of life's tests is to bring us to this end – to speak to Hashem and to believe in Him. When a person suffers, yet fails to recognize the Divine providence and fails to believe that everything is for the best, then he has suffered for nothing. Even worse, when he doesn't seek Hashem's help or seize the opportunity to get closer to Hashem, then his suffering becomes a ruined opportunity and therefore pointless. Pointless suffering causes sorrow to Hashem. Hashem wanted the person to use the difficult situation as a growth opportunity. But, when a person fails to seek Hashem and emuna, the golden growth opportunity is wasted and turns into pointless suffering.

The World is Full of His Glory

If we truly know that there is no one other than Hashem and that everything is from Him, then there's no concealment! How? Any concealment or apparent disappearance of Hashem is within a person's cognizance. If a person sees Hashem in everything, then where's the concealment? It doesn't exist! Hashem is everywhere all the time!

One must believe that Hashem is everywhere. Nothing is random in the world, but precisely directed with no mistakes. On the contrary, everything little occurrence in our lives is a tailor-made garment that fits us perfectly, designed to help us do our task in the world and to correct what needs correcting.

For a person to escape the darkness of concealment, there's no other choice but to tirelessly seek emuna. In reality, concealment is none other than a blemish in spiritual awareness and a figment of a person's mind. The only way to end the concealment is to pray for emuna and beg Hashem for spiritual awareness, to *know* that Hashem is everywhere and doing everything for the very best. The more one prays to Hashem, the better one gets to know Hashem. When we get to know Hashem and attain real emuna, there is no more concealment.

And he asked, "How can I get you out of here?"

Here the viceroy made a mistake. If he were a commando on a mission, his commander would have growled, "What are you asking questions for? You found her? Grab her and run! Complete the mission! Just as the obstacles didn't deter you on the way in to the castle, they shouldn't deter you now on the way out." During the debriefing, the viceroy would have been reprimanded for not grabbing the princess's hand and trying to escape.

Asking needless questions is an indication of incomplete emuna. Even our forefather Abraham asked a question that was superfluous for a *tzaddik* of his lofty spiritual level (see Bereishit, chapter 15):

"Hashem, how will I know that I will inherit the land?" Shortly thereafter, Hashem tells Abraham that his offspring will be slaves in a foreign land. Our sages tell us that the outcome of Abraham's sliver of doubt and his question was the bondage of his offspring in Egypt. Here in our tale as well, a moment of doubt and hesitation causes a lengthy delay in the redemption of the lost princess.

Emuna without Doubts

The slightest doubt in what we should be doing is a deficiency of emuna. As here in the tale, if the viceroy would have known without a doubt that Hashem wanted him to rescue the princess immediately, he would have ignored any obstacle and overcome any trepidation to perform his mission and thus bring the *geula*, or redemption.

Lack of firm conviction is a deficiency of emuna. Why? If one's emuna is complete, knowing that Hashem wants him to do a certain thing or act a certain way, then nothing else in the world matters. When juxtaposed with Hashem's will, everything else is null and void! If Hashem wants the princess rescued, then there're no walls, no guards, and no *Sitra Achra*, for nothing can stand in Hashem's way. That's how King David can declare so forcefully (Psalms 118:10), "All the nations surround me – in the Name of Hashem, I cut them down!"

King David was positive that even if all the nations of the world with millions of hostile troops would descend upon Jerusalem and surround him – he would rely on Hashem's Name! He would depend completely on emuna. He would mow them down like grass. Now we understand how King David can declare (ibid, 23), "Though I walk in the valley of death, **I shall not fear**, for You are with me..." With complete emuna, there is no fear, no matter what.

Rebbe Nachman of Breslov elaborates on this concept with the following tale (see Likutei Moharan II:46), told in the name of his great grandfather the Baal Shem Tov:

break through

"A king placed a treasure box in a certain place, and surrounded it with an optical illusion of great and mighty walls. People drew near and saw what seemed to them to be real walls that were difficult to breach. Some of them retreated on the spot. Others broke down the first wall, but couldn't break down the second wall. Still others broke down subsequent walls, but not all of them. Then came the king's son, who said: "I know that the walls are only an illusion; in reality, there are no walls." So he walked with confidence, until he passed them all. From here, the wise can understand the moral that all the obstacles and all the temptations and all the incitements [of the Evil Inclination – LB] are like walls placed around the treasure of *yirat Shamaim*, the fear of God, which are in actuality nothing. The important thing – a strong and brave heart, for then there are no obstacles. Particularly, the obstacles of materialism, such as: money, or obstacles from his wife, children, in-laws or parents and so forth, they are all nullified in the face of a heart that is strong and brave in the Name of Hashem. Even the might of heroes stems from a strong heart that is not afraid of contact in battle."

And she answered, "It's impossible for you to get me out of here…"

Since the viceroy expressed a hint of doubt with his question, revealing a deficiency of emuna, the princess answered: "It's impossible for you to get me out of here," for you still ask questions. She seems to be telling him that as long as the walls, the guards, or anything else other than Hashem deters him, he won't be able to get her out.

hinder

But, hope is never lost:

"…**U**nless you choose a place, and dwell there a full year. And the whole year, you must yearn to take me out. Any time that you have free, you should only yearn and pray and hope to free me. And you should fast frequently, and on the last day of the year, you should fast and not sleep the entire day."

The princess says to the viceroy: Since you're still asking questions, you clearly haven't prayed enough yet. So, go pray and yearn that emuna should be a part of you until you *know* that there is nothing other than Hashem and that everything is under His power. Even the *Sitra Achra* – the foolish old king - has no power and is nothing. On the contrary, if your emuna will be steadfast, even the dark side will fall at your feet and help you. So, go work for another whole year on your emuna, and then, you'll be able to get me out of here. One must yearn with a burning desire in order to attain emuna. Desire is the key word...

Chapter Eight

The Eyes

So he went and did just that. On the last day of the year, he fasted, and did not sleep, and rose and began the journey back. And on the way he saw a tree, and on it grew very appealing apples. And they were irresistibly tantalizing to his eyes...

deceive

The viceroy follows the princess's instructions to the letter: He chooses a place and goes there, utilizing every waking moment to pray and yearn for emuna, and to strengthen himself for his task. On the last day of the year, he fasts just like he was told to.

After he has done everything that the princess has told him to, nothing is left for him to do other than return to the princess and rescue her from captivity. At that moment, on the verge of redemption, the Evil Inclination overcomes him and knocks him down. Where does the downfall of the viceroy begin? From the eyes...

The Eye Sees and the Heart Covets

Rabbi Zev "Velvel" Cheshin of blessed memory, one of the prominent Breslover Chassidim of the previous generation, would say in the name of the Zohar that the *Yetzer Hara* is not allowed to enter a person except through the eyes. In our tale, we see this principle clearly. Had the viceroy guarded his eyes – and that means closing them, especially to temptation – he wouldn't have suffered a setback and he'd have rescued the princess then and there.

The very first sin in the world – Adam's – began with the eyes, for it is written (see Bereishit, chapter 3), "And the woman **saw** that the tree is good for eating, for it was irresistible **in her eyes** and pleasingly enlightening so she took from its fruit and gave it also to her man with her and he ate."

All the blemishes imaginable – lust for women, lust for food, lust for money, coveting, jealousy, and many more – all begin with the eyes. Rashi teaches us (see his commentary of Parshat Shlach), that "what the eye sees, the heart covets." This is literally a law of nature – whenever the eye sees something appealing, the heart immediately covets it, and the person is subjugated by the *Yetzer Hara*. Once the *Yetzer Hara* seizes control, a person is liable to commit every transgression imaginable. When we guard our eyes, we're spared from all this trouble, for what we don't see, we don't covet.

Let's go a step further: Hate, slander, greed, and confusion all start from the eyes as well. When one stares at others, and compares himself with them, he oftentimes belittles them to make himself feel better. Few people are satisfied with what they have when they look at their neighbors.

The First Choice

A person's first free-will choice in life is the eyes – whether to open them or to close them. If a person doesn't close his eyes, he loses his free will, for he'll fall prey to the *Yetzer Hara* and to all kinds of temptations and bodily urges. Closing ones eyes is the only way to avoid coveting; only then does one gain the free choice of thinking about Hashem or falling into a state of arrogance. This choice doesn't exist while the eyes are darting from one object to another. As we said, "the eye sees and the heart covets; when the heart covets something forbidden, it becomes spiritually defiled. Such impurity – the result of thoughts - is often worse than a forbidden act itself.

Therefore, one only has choice when the eyes are closed. Then, the choice is between thinking about Hashem, that there is no one other than Him, for He gives us the ability to see, among other things, or falling into a state of arrogance, thinking: "What a *tzaddik* I am!

Look how I walk around with my eyes closed!" and so forth.

When a person doesn't close his eyes, free choice doesn't even begin. Such a person loses connection with his ultimate purpose in life, for he surely forgets Hashem because of all that his eyes have seen. Each one of us must arouse ourselves and strengthen ourselves on this point. Even in places where we're permitted to open our eyes, we need extensive Divine mercy in order to prevent this world from confusing us and in order to cling to Hashem constantly. By opening one's eyes, one literally places himself into a state of concealment – nothing could be a greater tragedy.

The Internal Dimension of Guarding One's Eyes

The internal dimension of guarding one's eyes is emuna, when one says to himself, "I live my life with Hashem, there is no one other than Him, what else is there to see?" Such an individual realizes that every thought, utterance, and deed in life should be according to Hashem's will. Since Hashem commanded us to close our eyes, then that's exactly what we should do! Rabbi Eliahu Lapian of blessed memory said that our forefather Abraham didn't lift his eyes from his immediate two square meters all the days of his life. When describing the *Akeda*, the sacrifice of Isaac (see Bereishit 22:4), the Torah says, "And Abraham lifted his eyes on the third day, and saw the place from afar," in other words, Abraham lifted his eyes to see the cloud of the *Shechinah*, the Divine Presence, atop of Mount Moriah.

The next time Abraham lifted his eyes was to take the sacrificial ram that was sent to him in place of Isaac (*ibid, verse 13*): "And Abraham lifted his eyes and saw, and behold a different ram was entangled by the horns in the brambles, and Abraham went and took the ram, and raised it on the altar as a sacrifice in lieu of his son."

"And Abraham lifted his eyes on the third day, and saw the place…" Our sages teach that the place, in Hebrew *hamakom*, alludes to the Divine Presence. Abraham's heart was unified; there was no difference between his thoughts and his external actions. On an internal dimension, he only wanted to see Hashem. Therefore, when he lifted his eyes, that's exactly what he saw – Hashem!

In contrast, let's look at Esau. The Torah also says (*ibid, chapter 33*) that Esau "lifted his eyes." But what did he see? "...and he saw the women." Esau guarded his eyes, for he grew up in the home of a great *tzaddik*, his father Isaac. But, his heart harbored nothing but lewd thoughts. So, as soon as he lifted his eyes, he saw women. Hashem takes us on the road that we choose for ourselves.

Rabbi Yaakov Abu Chatzeira of blessed memory asks: If everything begins with the eyes, the why did the Torah mention the heart before it mentioned the eyes, for it is written, "You shall not stray after the heart and the eyes that you are pandering after them" (Bamidbar, ch. 15).

The answer is simple and quite self-apparent: When a person lives with emuna, he surely closes his eyes, so there's no need to command him to close his eyes. But, the heart incites a person to open his eyes, therefore the heart must be commanded first, as it is written, "You shall not stray after the heart and the eyes."

Because of the heart's role in tempting a person, the Torah also commands (Devarim, ch. 11), "Beware lest your heart tempt you to stray and serve false gods and bow down to them." The Baal Shem Tov of blessed memory explains that as soon as the heart tempts – in other words, a person allows himself to be tempted by the heart – immediately one strays and serves false gods, for he loses his connection with emuna. Losing one's emuna is tantamount [equal] to idol worship, for in spirituality, there's no middle ground.

What are You Looking For? [brave]

The viceroy made a valiant [brave] effort to rescue the princess – he traversed the desert and outback for years until he finally found her in the castle. Even then, his job wasn't over, for he still had an entire year of yearning, praying, and spiritual strengthening ahead of him. He did everything he was supposed to do until the climactic final day when he didn't sleep and didn't eat. He invested tremendous effort. Now, just as it comes time to rescue the princess – boom! He fell on his face in utter failure! He opened his eyes!

Can you imagine if this were a football game? People would be yelling from the grandstands, **"Hey, Mr. Viceroy! You're going to rescue the princess! She's emuna! Close your eyes! Concentrate on your goal! What are you looking for, other than emuna?!"**

A person looks around like his neck is a tank turret when he thinks there's anything in the world other than Hashem. If that's the case, then he's not yet ready to redeem the princess, for if he had emuna, he wouldn't look at anything. *small towers*

Ask yourself: what are you looking for in life? Do you want emuna? Do you want to know that there is nothing other than Hashem? Then why do you walk around with your eyes wide open? What's there to see? Are you going somewhere? Try to get there without forgetting Hashem on the way…

A Monumental Tzaddik – and Guardian of the Eyes

Rebbe Nachman teaches (Likutei Moharan I:67), that by guarding the eyes, one sifts the good from the evil in one's character by guarding the eyes. As long has one hasn't separated the good from the evil, then every time he opens his eyes, evil has an influence, leading to jealousy, hate, and lust. And, when someone sees something expressly forbidden, then the evil literally overcomes his soul, controlling all the limbs of his body; this is the reason that negative emotions have such a profound influence on physical health.

Only when one sifts the good from the evil within one's own character – strengthening the good and discarding the evil – can he open his eyes with no danger. Rebbe Nachman of Breslov reached such lofty spiritual heights that in his eyes there was no difference between a tree and a woman. Yet, he nevertheless guarded his eyes.

Other great *tzaddikim* who totally rid themselves of evil were extremely cautious about guarding their eyes nonetheless. The renowned *tzaddik* of the previous generation, Rabbi Yisrael Abu Chatzeira the beloved "Baba Sali" of blessed memory, maintained an exalted level of holiness, particularly in everything that had to do with the eyes. Now, if the great *tzaddikim* – who had totally rid themselves of evil – were so careful about guarding their eyes, shouldn't we? Since our own Evil Inclinations seek to trip us every step of the way, we should certainly be careful about guarding our eyes and denying evil the power to subdue us.

Chapter Nine

Deep Sleep

deceive

A nd on the way he saw a tree, and on it grew very appealing apples. And they were irresistibly tantalizing to his eyes, so he approached and ate one. Right after eating the apple, he dropped and fell asleep...

Rebbe Nachman writes (Likutei Moharan I:60, which is an elaboration of our tale at hand), that there are those that fall into a deep sleep because of improper eating. Specifically, he says:

"There are those who sleep their entire lives, even though they think that they are serving Hashem, praying and learning Torah, but despite all their work, Hashem has no gratification from them, for their deeds remain below, and lack the power to ascend.

"The principle vitality is the mind, for it is written: 'Wisdom shall revive its host,' (Ecclesiastes, ch. 7). When a person's service of Hashem is with the mind, it gains the vitality to ascend. But, when the mind falls into a state of constriction, tantamount to dormancy, then one cannot ascend.

"There are those who have fallen into a deep sleep by way of bodily lusts and evil deeds. There are those who are fine and upright people, but they fall because of eating. For sometimes when one eats a certain food that hasn't properly been purified for human consumption, the brain falls into slumber. Just as from a bodily standpoint there are those foods that make a person drowsy and those foods that arouse a person, so it is in spirituality, there are foods that haven't properly been purified on a spiritual level, that reduce a person to a state of spiritual slumber..."

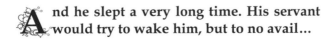

A nd he slept a very long time. His servant would try to wake him, but to no avail...

If a person doesn't arouse himself, then nothing else will arouse him. As much as the servant tried to wake the viceroy, he didn't succeed. We always have free choice, and our principle free choice is that we stimulate ourselves to search for truth. Without such self-stimulation - even in the slightest – neither Torah nor rote observance of mitzvot and the influence of *tzaddikim* will arouse a person. Rebbe Nachman says:

"One must awaken the sleeper, and it's impossible to arouse the sleeper until he awakens himself, for one must have stimulation from below" [self arousal, as opposed to depending on stimulation from above, or Divine arousal – LB].

Afterwards, he awoke from his sleep, and asked the servant, "Where am I in the world?"

A person wakes from spiritual slumber the minute he or she begins asking questions about life: What's my purpose on earth? Why do I feel a gnawing deficiency in my life? Why don't I have satisfaction and happiness? Shall I waste my life on things of no consequence? These questions arouse a person and bring him or her closer to the true purpose of life. As such, as soon as the viceroy awakens, he asks where he is in the world.

And the servant told him the story...

After the viceroy awoke, what is known in Kabbala as *itaruta dilatata*, or self arousal, the servant told him the "story." Allegorically, the servant told him tales of yesteryear to help the viceroy's reawakening. Rebbe Nachman writes (*ibid*), "Only when he arouses himself, can outside stimulation prevent him from further slumber."

When a person falls into spiritual sleep, in other words, when he loses focus on his purpose in life and therefore loses his connection with emuna – then he must be aroused by tales of yesteryear. Before Rebbe Nachman would tell his tales, he'd say, "Now I shall begin to tell a tale." His intention was that no conventional Torah lesson could wake his listeners from their spiritual slumber, only a tale. Within his tales were the loftiest esoteric secrets of Torah, for even the great Kabbalists testified that all the principles of Kabbala are alluded to in Rebbe Nachman's tales.

Facial Illumination   *summary*

Rebbe Nachman further explains that when a person falls into spiritual slumber, he loses his facial illumination, his Divine image. A person that falls into spiritual slumber falls from emuna and from the seventy faces of Torah, for emuna is the mind and wisdom of Torah. Since a person's wisdom illuminates his face, a fall from emuna   the epitome of wisdom   means losing one's facial illumination. With no facial illumination, one has no countenance at all. Therefore, to awaken a person, he must be shown his facial illumination, in other words, the emuna that can illuminate his mind and soul. But, as Rebbe Nachman teaches, this holy illumination must be clothed within a seemingly-mundane tale and not in a conventional Torah lesson, for the following reasons:

1. When curing a blind person, he must be shown light gradually, little by little, for a sudden illumination will be blinding. The Chassidic tale is in effect a garment that reduces the illumination of spiritual arousal. A person that might not be capable of absorbing a Torah ethics lecture can certainly listen to and be influenced by a tale.

2. The light of the *tzaddik*'s message must be clothed within a tale to hide it from the dark-side elements, to prevent them from clinging to such high-level holiness.

3. The dark-side forces that influence a person who's trapped in spiritual slumber won't allow him to listen to a Torah lesson; but, they won't prevent him from listening to tales about blacksmiths, horses, and the like. The Chassidic tale in which the Rebbe hides an inner meaning brings a person to Torah and to emuna without stimulating the resistance of the dark side.

Apparently, the tale has no connection to the Torah. The dark forces of evil (a person's own Evil Inclination) are caught off guard; they don't care if he listens to *bubba mysis*, old grandma's tales all day long. But, within the words of the *tzaddik*'s tales are hidden the light of arousal that stimulates a person to *teshuva* and to yearning for Hashem, so he can break free of the *Yetzer's* grasp.

A **nd the servant told him the story: "You were sleeping a very long time, several years. And I survived on the fruit..."**

Here, a nagging question arises: The viceroy fell asleep from his eating; the servant ate from the same fruit. Why didn't he fall asleep too?

The answer is, as we indicated earlier, that the servant alludes to the soul, and the soul doesn't "fall asleep," for it continues to be the life source that vitalizes a person. Even when the soul is in a period of stagnation, or spiritual slumber, outwardly it seems that the person is still awake, speaking, acting, and functioning. He could even be learning Torah or going through the motions of praying, even though he's spiritually dormant. Like Rebbe Nachman said, there are those that sleep their days away, even though they think they're serving Hashem, learning Torah, and praying...

A person in a spiritual deep sleep is certainly alive from a biological standpoint; such a person derives his low-level animal vitality from bodily amenities and passing enjoyments. Nevertheless, that person's *neshama*, or inner Divine soul, is not getting what it needs and therefore sinks into a deep sleep. With no connection to emuna, the *neshama* sleeps; the bodily shell seems alive, but in actuality, it's in a state of walking dormancy. In Rebbe Nachman's terms, such people "sleep their days away."

The concept of sleep belongs to the *neshama*, for when the *neshama* doesn't illuminate a person, she doesn't share with that person all the wonderful things that are happening to her every minute. The *neshama* enjoys sublime glimpses of Divine wisdom every single second; one's body clouds the messages transmitted from the *neshama*. The thicker and more crass the body, the less the *neshama* illuminates.

Chapter Ten

There's No Sadness in the World

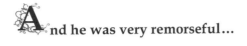

nd he was very remorseful...

Apparently, the viceroy's remorse is clearly understandable: He invested tremendous effort in locating the princess, and once he finally found her, he was forced to complete another year of extreme effort. And here, at the very last minute, he failed! What a disappointment!

In truth, sadness and remorse are major blemishes in emuna. The viceroy must understand that if he has not yet succeeded in redeeming the princess, he's not yet worthy of redeeming the princess. He still needs more prayer and more emuna to fulfill his task.

The proof is that the viceroy went to rescue the princess with open eyes. **One can't obtain the princess – emuna – with open eyes!**

It's impossible to rescue emuna without being connected to emuna. Why open your eyes when there's nothing to see but Hashem? Our consolation to the viceroy is this: Since you're not yet on the level of emuna where you can redeem the princess, be happy that you didn't redeem her! Be happy that you now know your true spiritual level, namely, that you need more work. False success clouds judgment; be happy that you haven't fooled yourself. Keep on working and praying, and with desire, you'll eventually succeed.

Lifelong Work

Any remorse a person has stems from the fact that he's striving for the outcome rather than for the work. A person that desires to serve Hashem should be interested in the *service* and not in the results. He or she should simply **love to serve Hashem**. If the service of Hashem means more prayer and more effort, then he or she should be happy with that.

A goal-oriented person regards attaining his goal as the completion of his task. Afterwards, he thinks he can sit out on the beach and relax, because the work is over. In the service of Hashem, such an outlook is totally wrong, for there's always more work to do. As long as one lives, there's more to do. In that respect, the viceroy's remorse is unjustifiable. He's serving the king, and before he continues to a new task, he has more work to do at the present task. Why be sad?

The trials and challenges that are sent to a person are merely tests designed to show that person where he or she is really holding on the spiritual ladder. If Hashem helps us to succeed in our test, it's a sign that we've **reached and earned** a given spiritual level. Hashem knows that we won't rest there on our laurels, but will continue to work hard and strive for more. Hashem gives us challenges to uplift us, making us constantly strive for more, just as a coach makes his weightlifters lift a little more every day, so they'll get stronger and achieve new heights.

If a person doesn't succeed, there's no mistake – **he simply isn't prepared to pass the test. The fact that he was looking for results, reward, and relaxation means that he is not yet deserving of that particular spiritual level**. Therefore, Hashem doesn't enable him to succeed, so that he'll learn his proper place, namely, that he has much more work to do. Rather than falling into sadness, depression and disappointment, he should rise to the challenge, strengthen his prayers and yearning for Hashem, and make his best effort until Hashem helps him cling to a new and higher dimension of emuna. Only then, will he be ready to redeem the princess.

The Joy of Recognition

When a person doesn't succeed in one of life's tests, then he should thank Hashem profusely for not giving him false success, illusions of grandeur, and spiritual levels that he doesn't deserve. The greatest joy is recognizing one's own reality – where we stand and our task at hand. We should continue to serve Hashem with patience and perseverance, yearning and praying with joy and with complete faith until we achieve the next higher level that we're striving for. Once we're truly worthy, Hashem will give us our new *madrega*, or spiritual level, beautifully and wonderfully; we'll *know* that it comes from Hashem. As such, we won't feel conceited; we'll simply strive for more.

This is exactly what the princess is instructing the viceroy in the continuation of our tale: Go find a new place, stay there for a year, and so forth. The princess is telling the viceroy to continue praying and yearning, for experience has shown that his efforts haven't been adequate to accomplish the task at hand. Sadness and despair contribute nothing.

S **o he returned there and found her. And she revealed her great distress to him...**

The princess's sorrow, an allusion to the sorrow of the *Shechinah*, or Divine Presence, is not a blemish in emuna. Her sorrow is true sorrow, the sorrow of holiness that people are trapped in darkness so far away from emuna that they can't see Hashem's magnificent Divine Providence over all of His creations.

In truth, were it not for the viceroy's sorrow, the princess wouldn't have been distressed at all. Her only sorrow is the concealment. If the viceroy would have believed that his failure was also from Hashem, then the continuation of his task would have been much easier, and the princess wouldn't be so upset about him.

At every moment, a person has the free choice of clinging to Hashem and to emuna, for there's no place in the world where a person can't reach out for Hashem. Hashem is everywhere, even in the lowest and most desolate places on earth.

Therefore, when a person clings to the simple faith that everything comes from Hashem, then he's not in concealment at all. No matter how he falls or fails, if he believes that his setback comes from Hashem and continues to serve Hashem with joy, then Hashem has no sorrow. Hashem's only sorrow is when people don't believe that everything is from Him and for the very best – failures, setbacks, ups, downs, everything!

> "**I**f you had only come on the prescribed day, you would have taken me out of here. And because of one day, you lost..."

Here, Rebbe Nachman of Breslov is alluding to a passage in Psalm 95, "Today, if you heed His voice," which he elaborates in Likutei Moharan I:272, as follows:

"'Today, if you heed His voice,' is an important guideline in the service of Hashem, that one should not look at anything other than the day at hand. Both in the business of making a living and seeking ones needs, one shouldn't think from one day to the next, as our holy books say. The same goes for the service of Hashem. One should not regard anything other than that particular day and that particular hour. For when a person desires to enter in the service of Hashem, it seems to be a heavy weight that's impossible to carry. But, when one thinks only of the day at hand, he doesn't have a heavy load at all, and also won't push things off from today until tomorrow, saying: Tomorrow I'll begin, tomorrow I'll pray earnestly, and so forth with other tasks. A person has nothing in his world other than the particular day and hour at hand, for tomorrow is an entirely different world. 'Today, if you heed His voice,' – 'today' specifically, and understand."

When a person is occupied with something, whether a mundane task or a spiritual one, he should concentrate on the present task and not think about anything else. Rebbe Nathan of Breslov instructed his son Yitzchak, who worked as a postal clerk and was confused about the best way of meeting all his obligations, the best way to serve Hashem. He said: "When you work at the post office, concentrate on your work, to prevent mistakes. But, the minute you leave the post office, forget completely about your work and focus all your thoughts on Hashem and on His Divine service."

Rebbe Nathan also wrote that this advice was the only way that

Rebbe Nachman succeeded in accomplishing what he accomplished (see Shivchei Haran, 14):

"His daily workload was enormous and very difficult. It was so difficult that he could barely withstand the heaviness of the yoke of his responsibilities. Only by this advice could he continue with his work, namely, that each day, he'd think that he had no other concerns other than that particular day, and that way, he could carry the weight of that day's responsibilities. For a person is capable of doing anything in the world on one particular day, since it's only a single day; then, on the morrow, he would only look at that day.

"He acted this way always, never thinking about anything but that particular day, and that way, he could carry the load that was so heavy. Without this, he couldn't have withstood the strain of his many activities in the service of Hashem, each done with tremendous strain and effort, which would have added up to an impossible load. The only way he succeeded was with this advice – not to think of anything other than that particular day."

This is what the princess says to the viceroy: "And because of **one day**, you lost." Since your service of Hashem wasn't **"one day,"** in other words, since you didn't focus exclusively on the day at hand, you failed. You only have today – nothing else – so concentrate on your present task. If you'd have focused on what you were supposed to do, you wouldn't have strayed aside to eat a forbidden apple, and you would have redeemed me.

Don't Worry about Tomorrow

"Today, if you heed His voice," the principle of taking each day at a time is the key to serving Hashem properly and winning the war against the *Yetzer Hara*. With one day at a time, one can withstand any hardship. Also, when trying to overcome a temptation, bad habit, or a bodily urge, it's much easier to succeed by taking each hour at a time and each day at a time. Once the *Yetzer Hara* has been repelled for a short duration, it will leave completely.

An old Arab expression says that if you load a camel's back straw by straw, then the camel can carry five bales. But, if you drop a bale on its back all at once, you'll break its back. In like fashion, the *Yetzer Hara* shows a person that he or she won't be able to withstand such a lengthy test or tribulation; the person then falls into despair, quits, and surrenders to the *Yetzer Hara* before the battle even started. But, if the same person would take heart and tell himself that he certainly can beat the *Yetzer Hara* for one hour or one day, then he could probably withstand and overcome a much more severe test than the one at hand.

The Zohar mentions the principle of taking each hour and each day at a time in the service of Hashem and says that if the Children of Israel would have succeeded in delaying the unfortunate fiasco of the golden calf for even a few minutes, then they would have succeeded in avoiding it altogether. It says that Aaron should have tried to delay the whole thing for even a few minutes by letting the gold drop from his fingers or some other ploy. By delaying temptation for a few minutes, one can totally avoid a transgression.

Normally, a test lasts only for a few minutes, especially when it comes to bodily drives and appetites. This is especially so in the case of anger, for if one can succeed in maintaining focus for a few seconds without losing one's temper, then the wave of anger passes by like a fleeting cloud. The same thing goes for a temptation to breach one's holiness; by delaying an unholy act for a few minutes, one can easily maintain personal holiness all the time.

Living the Moment

The same principle applies in all aspects of Divine service such as praying with intent or learning with diligence. It's hard to do either for a lengthy period of time, but one can do both by concentrating on the moment at hand. When we tell ourselves that *now* we can pray with proper intent, then the prayer doesn't seem like a heavy weight on our shoulders. But, when we fail to concentrate on the current moment, then our minds begin to wander from past to future, sailing the four corners of the earth. When one looks at the coming four-hour Talmud-study session, he might feel a heaviness or laziness. But, by learning earnestly for a minute at a time, the hours fly by productively.

Pondering the difficulties of the past and the trepidations of the future weaken and incapacitate a person. Such thoughts make meeting the slightest challenges difficult. When a person fails to deal with the current moment, he or she certainly can't perform a necessary task with joy and success.

All the confusion and misdirection that people suffer from stems from the fact that they don't live the moment at hand, and fail to realize that there's nothing in the world that matters other than the current moment. Why? The past is gone, the future is not yet here, and the present transpires with the blink of an eye. Who cares what'll be in another minute? Why waste the present minute? Each moment that we properly utilize accumulates to a life of success and gratification.

Today Moshiach Will Come

The Midrash (Yalkut Shimoni, Psalms) tells a story of Rabbi Yehoshua ben Levy meeting Eliahu HaNavi (Elija the Prophet). Rabbi Yehoshua ben Levy asked, "When will Moshiach come?"

Eliahu HaNavi answered, "Go ask him yourself," and showed him where to find Moshiach.

Rabbi Yehoshua ben Levy approached Moshiach and asked, "When does my lord plan to come?"

Moshiach answered, "Today!"

The next day, when Rabbi Yehoshua ben Levy saw that Moshiach had not yet arrived, he returned to Eliahu HaNavi complaining that Moshiach had broken a promise to come today, for he failed to come. Eliahu HaNavi answered that Moshiach's intent was that "today" means "Today, if you heed His voice." For in truth, Moshiach is ready to come every single day, and the only delay is our failure to serve Hashem minute by minute according the principle of "Today, if you heed His voice," as we've just explained.

This is what the princess is telling the viceroy: "If you had only come on the prescribed day, you would have taken me out of here. And because of **one day**, you lost." In other words, if you would have done your task minute by minute according the principle of "Today, if you heed His voice," then your personal savior would have come already. If the entire world would serve Hashem in this manner, then Moshiach would certainly come and we'd be redeemed this very minute.

> **N**evertheless, it is very difficult not to eat, especially on the last day, when the Evil Inclination is very overpowering. (In other words, the princess told him that now she would make the conditions more lenient, that from now he would not be expected to fast, for that is a very hard condition to fulfill, etc.)...

The above passage is an allusion to the principle that Rebbe Nachman teaches us, namely, that one should not fast other than the prescribed public fasts that are mentioned in the Shulchan Aruch. Former generations incorporated fasts and all types of self-punishment in their self-purification efforts; Rebbe Nachman stopped all that, and taught us that an hour of personal prayer in seclusion can rectify more than all the fasts and self-punishments combined. One can attain lofty levels of spirituality by way of personal prayer. Rebbe Nachman even said about himself that had he known in his younger years the true power of personal prayer, he wouldn't have broken his body with continued and lengthy fasts like he did.

> **S**o now, choose a place again, and dwell there also a year, as before...

The princess sends the viceroy on an additional year's prayer mission. His lack of success indicates a lack of prayer that must be corrected before he can redeem the princess. Hashem's judgments are absolute justice; if a person has not yet succeeded, it's a clear indication that he or she is not yet worthy of success. In the case of the viceroy, his failure indicates that he deserves to fail, for he has not yet attained the spiritual level of worthiness to rescue the princess. But, if he now strengthens his prayers – both in quality and in quantity – he shall certainly be worthy of future success.

We should all learn this lesson: Our delay in achieving what we want to achieve is no mistaken judgment on Hashem's behalf; it shows that we haven't prayed enough. Therefore, the key to success is more prayer. As soon as we fulfill the prayer quota for a certain request, we'll see with our own eyes how obstacles fall by the wayside and we achieve what we have set out to achieve, particularly if our goal is a spiritual one.

Chapter Eleven

Don't Be a Drunk

nd on the last day you will be allowed to eat. Only you must not sleep, and must not drink wine, so you won't fall asleep. For the essential thing is not to sleep." So he went and did accordingly...

As we mentioned earlier, the princess eased the demands on the viceroy and this time allowed him to eat. She warned him, though, to stay clear of intoxicating beverages that sink a person into slumber, for the main thing is to stay awake. Rebbe Nachman teaches in several places that intoxication confuses one's powers of imagination and reduces a person to a state of material and spiritual slumber.

Our holy Rebbe commanded us to steer clear of *any* intoxicating beverages, including arak, whiskey, cognac, brandy, vodka, liqueurs, beer, wine, ale, and everything else with an alcoholic content except in the fulfillment of a mitzvah, such as drinking wine on Purim or Passover, when we make extensive spiritual preparation so that we can fulfill the mitzvah in complete holiness. Drug use is also out of the question, for heavy-drug users lose their human image.

Light Drugs

Particular dangerous are the so-called "light" drugs, which in certain respects are more harmful than the life-threatening heavy drugs. Users of light drugs think that they can still function normally, hold a job, maintain a marriage and family, and the like. The truth is that they destroy everything in their path including themselves. A person in the self-destruct mode can't stand the slightest challenge, stress, or pressure. He or she seeks a head-in-the-cloud existence with no demands and no responsibility. Light-drug users lose their inner strength and resolve, self-image, and motivational powers. They ultimately lose their jobs and their marriages, sowing seeds of misery wherever they go, Heaven forbid.

Unfortunately, light drugs have become so widespread that some people insist that their various substances help them attain sensations of uplifting, inspiration, and other nonsense. Any drug-induced sense of being uplifted or inspired is none other than the alien fires of the *Sitra Achra*, or dark side of spirituality.

Alien Fire

We learn in *Parshat Shemini* (see Vayikra, chapter 10): "The sons of Aaron, Nadav and Avihu, each took his fire pan and they put fire in them and placed incense on it [the fire - LB], and they brought before Hashem an **alien fire** that He had not commanded them. A fire came forth from Hashem and consumed them, and they died in front of Hashem."

Our sages examine the sin of Nadav and Avihu, and write that Nadav and Avihu wanted to serve Hashem under the influence of alcohol. They certainly weren't drunkards; on the contrary, they were *tzaddikim* of the highest level. Their mistake was that they believed they could attain even higher spiritual heights by way of substance usage.

Hashem doesn't want "spiritual heights" that result from the alien fire of outside substances like wine, liquor, and drugs of all sorts. These are the alien fires that Hashem doesn't want. Hashem wants our spiritual gain that results from yearning, dedication, perseverance, and hard work. With proper effort, we merit a fire from Heaven that kindles in our hearts in the holy love and enthusiasm for Divine service. Such a fire is complete holiness, free of any impurity or alien influence.

No to Tobacco

Even cigarettes are light drugs, for nicotine is a habit-forming substance. Smokers have the illusion that smoking calms them and helps them to think. Spiritually and physiologically, nothing could be further from the truth. Smoking seriously constricts blood vessels, and hampers the flow of blood to the brain and heart that is so necessary for a calm and a clear mind. Smoking destroys the heart and the lungs and endangers a person's health. Hashem has no gratification from a person smoking.

Cigarettes, like other light drugs, enslave people, consuming both their money and their health. Rebbe Nachman forbade tobacco consumption on behalf of his disciples. He said that it's not befitting for a servant of Hashem to smoke. He asked rhetorically, "Don't we have enough bodily urges without adding tobacco?"

The thought of a servant of Hashem that requires inhalation and exhalation of smoke to attain vitality is disparaging. It's also a defamation of Hashem's Name and a gross insult to Torah and mitzvot, as if to say that Torah and mitzvot are not enough to satisfy a person, Heaven forbid. Also, the smoker violates the commandment to protect and preserve his own health. Even worse, researchers have proven that smokers endanger others, forcing them to inhale secondary smoke. What gives them the right to cause damage to other people, oftentimes to their own spouses and children?

Even if a person doesn't see himself as a servant of Hashem, anyone with the slightest common sense realizes that smoking holds no benefits, only damage. Any smoker should take an honest look at himself and say no to tobacco. Suffering a few days of nicotine withdrawal is far preferable to a life of suffering and enslavement to tobacco.

On the last day, he would go there, and saw a spring flowing, with a reddish hue and a wine-scented fragrance. He asked the servant, "Did you see that spring, which should have water in it, but its color is red, and its scent is of wine?" And he went and sipped from the spring. And he immediately fell into a sleep that lasted several years - seventy, to be exact...

The *Yetzer Hara* is a crafty fox; when he sees that a person is pursuing the path of holiness and avoiding even the slightest of transgressions, he gives that person an enticing or tempting thought of something extraordinary, calling him or her to come closer and have a look. Once the unsuspecting individual draws closer, he or she falls into the Yetzer's trap.

prove to be incorrect   *go slowly*

Rebbe Nachman warns (see Sefer HaMidot, Adultery, 10): Don't negotiate with a temptation, for the lingering thought of a temptation – even refuting it – arouses the desire for that temptation.

Again, we see that the viceroy has not yet attained the level of emuna. What's he looking at the spring for? What does he care if water or wine flows in the spring? Indeed, even if it is wine, the princess commanded not to drink wine, so why think twice? It turns out that the viceroy's main mistake was his failure to compose himself and clarify the truth in his mind. Without a strong stance on the truth, he fell.

The viceroy's second fall is much more serious than his first, for this fall led to a seventy-year slumber. Interestingly, the Hebrew gematria, or numerical value for wine, *yayin*, is seventy! Wine and light drugs are enough to sever a person completely from the seventy faces of Torah.

Also, alcohol and drug addiction – functional addiction included – occupies the addicted person 24 hours a day, not leaving a single minute for self composure and introspection.   *examine of one's thought*

Drinkers and 'light' drug-users fail to function properly for several reasons: Since their acts are against the law and unacceptable in greater society, they must hide what they do. Also, since their actions aren't acceptable in wholesome circles, users befriend fringe elements of society that act like they do, and are even more negatively influenced by them. In a nasty downward spiral, their incomes suffer, their families suffer, and they walk a path of eventual self-destruction.

From Above

More than once, the viceroy almost rescued the princess. He reached the gate of salvation, and fell. Each time, he fell at the very last minute. His failure comes from above, for Rebbe Nachman writes (Likutei Moharan I: 261): "When a person falls from his spiritual level, he should know that the fall comes from above." In other words, the lack of success in passing a test means a lack of assistance from above. Without Hashem's help, a person falls.

No one is capable of withstanding any trial or tribulation without help from above. Our sages teach that a person's Evil Inclination overcomes him every day, and without Hashem's help, the person would be subdued. When a person makes what *he thinks* to be his best effort to get close to Hashem, to make *teshuva*, and to overcome his bodily appetites and bad habits – yet he still falls from time to time – he should know that he's not being helped from above, **for his own good.**

Why didn't Hashem give a helping hand to the viceroy as he fell once more on his way to rescuing the princess? Why doesn't Hashem help us once and for all to overcome the *Yetzer Hara* and to rescue our own princess?

The main reason is that we are **not yet ready** to redeem our personal princess. If Hashem would give us unlimited success at this time, instantly, with no setbacks or delays, we'd probably become arrogant. Instant success gives a person the illusion that he's a *tzaddik*, or deserving, or Heaven's gift to mankind – he may even begin believing that he's the Moshiach! Instant success destroys yearning, for one who succeeds effortlessly doesn't have to pray and yearn to succeed. Instant success is liable to sink a person into spiritual slumber, thinking that he's already reached the pinnacle of righteousness. One who's smugly happy with himself doesn't strive for more.

Clearly, Hashem doesn't want us to fall into these kinds of traps. He wants to give us the gift of real success, not artificial silver-plated success. Artificial and instant success would be spiritually dangerous for us, for we might sleep or flounder at a low spiritual level thinking that we've already reached the peak of Mount Sinai. It turns out that all the obstacles and delays along our spiritual way are all for the best, to strengthen us until we reach the level where we really are worthy.

A person must wait patiently until he sees the fruit of his labors. Our sages say that one who wants to be purified is told to wait. What does a person do during the waiting period? Sleep? Eat ice-cream? No! He works hard at prayer! He learns Torah! He perfects his character! He yearns for Hashem and seeks His proximity!

One must therefore be strong and not discouraged no matter what happens to him – falls, setbacks, trials, tribulations, difficulties – anything! Life on this lowly earth is one continuous battle, and there's no choice but to fight. We must cling to our desires, yearn for Hashem, and try our very best to realize our dreams by praying constantly until we're really worthy of getting close to Hashem. We should always remember that our successes are from Hashem, and not credit ourselves for anything. That way, our hearts remain free of arrogance and we avoid spiritual slumber. One who desires more and more spirituality is one who really lives.

As soon as Hashem sees that a person is worthy, He sends help from above in completing the mission of rescuing the princess, as we see at the end of our tale.

The Sifting Process

A person comes to this world to perform a task. He's required to visit all the places where he stumbled in former reincarnations, and to meet those individuals with whom he must "sift" out a soul correction. He must withstand trials and tribulations that will help him attain his personal *tikkun*, or soul correction, thus contributing to the *tikkun* of the entire world. He won't be able to redeem his princess until he's completed all the other tasks on the way.

Sifting our own good from the evil within us, thus correcting ourselves and attaining our person *geula*, or redemption, is an integral part of the general *geula* of the entire world. As such, Rebbe

Nachman teaches (see Likutei Moharan I:5), that everyone should say: "The world was created just for me, therefore I'm responsible for the world, so I must attend to its needs and pray for it."

Sometimes a person is actually on the level of worthiness, but his personal *tikkun* is delayed because the world isn't yet ready. In that case, such a person should pray for the correction of the world, for the world's correction and his personal correction are intertwined.

One would be best advised to pray daily for the success of the Jewish people, for Jewish outreach, for the spread of Torah and *teshuva* in the world, and certainly for the redemption of the Jewish people, the ingathering of the exiles, and the rebuilding of our Holy Temple in Jerusalem. Praying for personal needs is not enough, especially when the world at large needs so much prayer and Divine mercy. Once again, the more a person contributes to the general redemption, the more he'll hasten his personal redemption.

If a person ignores the world's needs, and fails to pray for the general redemption and for the Jewish people as a whole, then he'll be hampered from above again and again; such an individual won't be allowed to complete his personal mission in rescuing his own princess.

Rebbe Nathan of Breslov said: "My Moshiach has come already!" In other words, Rebbe Nathan achieved his personal redemption, for he devoted his entire adult life to the general *tikkun* of the Jewish people with a level of self-sacrifice, dedication, perseverance and suffering that no words can describe. In his final days he wept that he didn't devote even more time to disseminating Rebbe Nachman's teachings in the world and writing more books based on Rebbe Nachman's wisdom, which certainly would have been of priceless benefit for the Jewish people.

I Fell, but I Got Up

We must all know one thing: Every setback in life – even a setback that results from our own mistake – comes from above!

Therefore, one should never torture oneself. There's no room to blame oneself or anybody else for troubles in life, and certainly not to fall into despair and depression. The important thing is desire; falling means nothing, as long as a person maintains a desire to do better. Never abandon your desires, for Hashem looks first and foremost at our desires. The best way to counter a fall or failure is to declare a new beginning and get back up on our feet as fast as possible. We desire to do better! The fall means nothing if we get back on our feet swiftly and with new resolve.

After a failure, a person is being tested; will he fall into despair and depression? Will he make a better second effort? How fast will he be back on his feet? When we utilize our fall to get up fast and to make a better second effort, then we turn a failure into a smashing success. That way, each of us is assured of achieving his or her complete personal *tikkun*.

Tremendous Reinforcement

Even more importantly, a person that falls yet gets up quickly gives much more gratification to Hashem than a person that never fell in the first place. Hashem wants our desire more than anything, and the biggest expression of desire is the manner that we pick ourselves up after a setback. OK, so we did something wrong? We did something that Hashem told us not to do? Let's not fret! From this moment on, let's decide that we're going to be better. We can return to Hashem with greater desire and greater yearning. We can overcome our faults and our bodily drives. Oftentimes the fall simply fuels our desire – that in itself is a triumph!

The entire *teshuva* process depends on the desire to do better, especially after a setback. People that have bounced back from setbacks attain a much higher spiritual level than those that have never suffered setbacks. So many people fail to realize the gratification that Hashem receives when a person makes a tremendous effort in reinforcing himself after a fall. Those who get stuck in self-pity, despair, depression, and disappointment never make proper *teshuva*. Sadness cannot be a vessel for holiness.

The *Yetzer Hara* is a liar. He tries to tell a person that he or she is doomed after a fall. Hopelessness disarms a person. But, a new start and a new resolve disarm the *Yetzer Hara*.

Knowing that our fall comes from above saves us from a low self image, feelings of guilt, and from self-persecution. The worry and anxiety of despair destroy a person's mental, physical, and spiritual health. Reinforcing ourselves after a setback and starting anew save us untold mental, physical, and spiritual wear and tear. The important thing is to get back on our feet as fast as possible.

Before we fall, we do everything in our power so that we don't fall. But, once we've fallen, it's a sign that Hashem wants us to strengthen ourselves. When we do, we've lost nothing and have gained everything – a tremendous new spiritual reinforcement!

Each fall is really a chance to attain new heights. The more we reinforce ourselves, the more we've taken advantage of a fall or setback as a growth tool.

Breslover tradition, handed down from teacher to pupil for the last two hundred years, teaches that in the future – after the sin of Adam is rectified – the world will be far more beautiful than it would have been had Adam never sinned. The same goes for the individual: the person that fearlessly recovers from a fall develops a depth of enhanced inner strength that those who have never fallen don't usually attain.

To Be a "Kosher" Person

Rebbe Nachman once said (see Chayei Moharan, 453): "Just as you see me, I mean to say, you all regard me as a complete *tzaddik*, even so, if Heaven forbid I were to commit the greatest sin in the world, even so, I wouldn't let the sin throw me off track, I'd just continue to be a kosher person after the sin as before the sin, only afterwards, I'd make *teshuva*!"

Apparently, Rebbe Nachman's saying is strange. How can a complete *tzaddik* like Rebbe Nachman say that after the sin he wouldn't be thrown off track, and that he'd continue to be a *tzaddik* as before the sin? Rebbe Nachman knew that if he would fall, he'd quickly climb to his feet with a new and burning desire to do better. As we learned in the beginning of this book, as soon as a person merely desires to do better, he's considered a complete *tzaddik*! So we see, that even after a nasty fall, a person can be a *tzaddik* as long as he or she maintains a strong desire to be better and to get closer to Hashem. All he or she has to do is to be happy and to make *teshuva* for whatever they did wrong.

Rebbe Nachman was also teaching his disciples the principle that we've been discussing in this chapter, namely, that a person after a fall can rise much higher than a person that never fell. Hashem loves strong comebacks. *Teshuva* depends on strong comebacks.

Each of us should decide that we'll always be "kosher" people, by constantly yearning for the proximity of Hashem. As long as we never give up our desires, we're assured a rosy future. Even if we slip up from time to time, we can make sameday or on-the-spot *teshuva* for whatever we did wrong. The important thing is to keep smiling and to keep trying.

We should internalize – deep in our hearts – a burning desire to get close to Hashem, like an eternal flame that can't be extinguished by the icy waters of a setback. Such a desire grants unfathomable gratification to Hashem. With the will to start anew and to rise quickly after a fall, a person will be stronger than if he or she had never fallen. This is the path of *teshuva* – a new and courageous start of getting to our feet speedily after a fall. Those who walk this path will surely redeem their own personal princess.

And great numbers of soldiers passed with their accompanied gear. The servant hid himself from the soldiers.

When a person falls into a state of spiritual slumber, until he awakens, he experiences all kinds difficulties, ups and downs, confusion, and the like. Rebbe Nathan wrote (Rebbe Nachman's Tales, Introduction): "During the time of spiritual slumber, Heaven forbid, a person suffers what he suffers, and that's the allusion of the great number of soldiers passing by while the viceroy was sleeping. 'Their accompanied gear' are all the tribulations that come along with a period of suffering."

> **A** fterwards came a covered carriage, and in it sat the princess. She stopped next to him. She descended and sat by him, recognizing who he was. She shook him strongly, but he failed to wake up. And she started to bemoan, "How many immense efforts and travails he has undergone, these many years, in order to free me, and because of one day that he could have freed me, and lost it...," and she cried a great deal about this, saying "There is great pity for him and for me, that I am here so very long, and cannot leave..."

This segment alludes to the fact that the *Shechinah*, the holy Divine Presence, is constantly trying to awaken people from their spiritual slumber. When a person fails to wake up, the *Shechinah* suffers indescribable anguish, for she has infinite compassion for every person, especially for the Jewish soul that's not aware of its own holiness and lofty spiritual status and continues to flounder in a spiritual exile. Such a soul sleeps its life away, wasting time on television, movies, inconsequential pastimes, and outright idleness. The sleeping soul forgets completely about its own Creator and the myriad of favors and miracles the Creator does for it every minute of the day. With emuna in exile, the soul slumbers, and the *Shechinah* wails.

> **A** fter that, she took her scarf off of her head, and wrote upon it with her tears, and laid it by him. And she rose and boarded her carriage, and rode away...

The scarf with the tears written on it is the teachings of the *tzaddik*, which are written in his tears. The words of the true *tzaddik* are like burning coals dipped in the tears of sorrow, for the true *tzaddik* feels the holy *Shechinah's* sorrow and the sorrow of the Jewish souls in exile. Before writing any Torah nuance or before lecturing, the *tzaddik* cries to Hashem begging for the right words that will stimulate readers and listeners to return to Hashem. The *tzaddik* has no other motive than bringing people closer to Hashem and spreading emuna and Hashem's glory in the world. Therefore, the words that flow forth from a heart that burns with the love of Hashem have the power to warm the hearts of those who read or listen to them.

Chapter Twelve

The Mountain of Gold

A fterwards, he awoke, and asked the servant, "Where am I in the world?" So he told him the whole story - that many soldiers had passed there, and that there had been a carriage, and a woman who wept over him and cried out that there is great pity on him and on her. In the midst of this, he looked around and saw that there was a scarf lying next to him. So he asked, "Where did this come from?" The servant explained that she had written upon it with her tears. So he took it and held it up against the sun, and began to see the letters, and he read all that was written there - all her mourning and crying as previously mentioned, and that she is no longer in the said castle, and that he should look for a mountain of gold and a castle of pearls, "There you shall find me..."

The princess informs the viceroy that she's no longer in the first castle and that he must now search for a mountain of gold and a castle of pearls – there he'll find her. The mountain of gold and castle of pearls metaphorically indicate our current exile – the exile of lust for money. Today, the *Shechinah* and emuna have fallen to an abyss in the lowest depths of the *kelipot*, the darkness of evil and impurity. This is what's known as the fiftieth gate, or lowest level of spiritual impurity, since the lust for money includes and encompasses every form of idolatry. Indeed, there is no idol worship more spiritually devastating than the lust for money. Rebbe Nachman's imagery of the mountain of gold and the castle of pearls represents "Idollartry" – the worst form of idolatry.

No generation in history has been so driven by the demon of money chasing as this generation. Few are those who don't suffer from the lust for money. In Rebbe Nachman's "Tale of the Master of Prayer", the master of prayer says that the lust for money is the worst of all, for it's almost impossible to uproot, as explained there.

Why is the lust for money so severe? All other lusts and bodily appetites such as the craze for eating or the preoccupation with sex are also damaging, and require massive effort to break free from them. But, there are times when a person doesn't think about them. For example, one who lusts for food doesn't think about food after a heavy meal. At that time, it's possible to discuss other things with him, such as faith and *teshuva*. Even those that succumb to a lust for sex don't think about their carnal drives 100% of the time.

But, when a person suffers from a lust for money, his mind is locked on money 24 hours a day. The moment he opens his eyes, he thinks about money, how to make money, how to accumulate more money, and so forth. All day long, he focuses on money. At night, he twists from side to side in bed thinking about money, dreaming new schemes of obtaining more money the next day. Such a person doesn't have a free moment to listen to anything about Hashem, the soul's needs, or spirituality.

When someone tries to speak to the money chaser about the ultimate purpose of life, the words fall on deaf ears and a hermetically-sealed heart. At best, the money chaser will listen politely for a few moments and nod his head. But, nothing will penetrate; the money chaser will think, "Hey, time is money? Why waste time on silly philosophical discussions when I can be making more money?!"

The Truly Rich Man

We therefore see that the mountain of gold and castle of pearls is the *tikkun* of this generation. In other words, our task is to break free from the chains of monetary lust. We do this by developing our trust in Hashem, by minimizing our material needs, and by being satisfied with what we have to the point that we feel like we live on a mountain of gold and in a castle of pearls that lack nothing, and contain all the riches in the world.

As long as we lack the emuna, trust, and happiness that impart the feeling that we live on a mountain of gold and in a castle of pearls that lack nothing, we won't be able to rescue the princess. Rebbe Nachman teaches that obtaining genuine emuna is impossible without shattering one's lust for money (see Likutei Moharan I:13).

So he left the servant behind, and went to look for her alone...

Here, the viceroy climbs another rung up the spiritual ladder. He leaves his servant behind – in other words, his basic animal soul – and proceeds to search for the princess. Here, we learn that the viceroy has cleansed himself of all animal drives and bodily appetites to the point where he is no longer concerned with his basic animal soul. The viceroy has uplifted his material aspirations to the loftier level of spiritual aspirations, yearning for emuna and the redemption from spiritual exile.

From this point on, the viceroy's search takes on a new dimension. As soon he turns his back on the mundane and material, shedding the drives of the flesh, his search becomes steadfast, perseverant, dedicated and focused. Nothing stands in his way as he courageously overcomes all obstacles. Even obstacles that come from formidable individuals fail to confuse or disorient him. He continues on his way until he finds the princess.

And he went for several years searching, and he composed himself, thinking that certainly a mountain of gold and a castle of pearls would not be found in a settled area, for he was an expert in the map of the world. So he went to the deserts. And he searched for her there many years...

Time and again we see how the different stages in the search for the princess require years of hard work. From here we learn that the search for emuna is a step-by-step process that requires patience, commitment, and perseverance. In spirituality, there are no instant results. Moving up the ladder of Divine service is a slow and lengthy process. We also see how in each new stage, the viceroy "composes himself" in personal prayer…

> **A**fterwards, he saw a giant man, far beyond the normal human proportions. He was carrying a massive tree, the size of which is not found in settled areas. The man asked him, "Who are you?" He answered, "I am a man." The giant was amazed, and exclaimed, "I have been in the desert such a long time, and I have never seen a man here." So he told him the whole story, and that he was searching for a mountain of gold and a castle of pearls. The giant answered him, "Certainly, it does not exist at all." And he discouraged him and said that they had muddled his mind with nonsense, for it surely does not exist. So he (the viceroy) started to cry bitterly, for he felt certain that it must exist somewhere. And this giant discouraged him, saying that certainly he had been told nonsense. Yet he (the viceroy) still said that it must exist…

The viceroy has now reached a spiritual level where he no longer has obstacles from his own bodily drives. He now faces obstacles in the form of outsiders, not even regular people but individuals of enormous proportions, which alludes to great *tzaddikim*. As it is hinted here, the viceroy meets a giant carrying a massive tree; this is an allusion to a tremendous Torah scholar, for the Torah is described metaphorically as a "tree of life," (see Proverbs, ch. 3).

Our holy Rebbe Nachman is teaching us that people are the greatest obstacles in our journey to truth. Here, the viceroy hasn't encountered some simple person, but a "giant", a *tzaddik* and a scholar of magnificent proportions, who is capable of ruling over the animals, the birds, and even the winds, as we see in the continuation of our tale.

These tremendous individuals are telling the viceroy that he's living a mistake! They say there's no such thing as a mountain of gold and a castle of pearls! In essence, they are telling him, "Listen, friend – we have attained lofty spiritual levels. We're telling you that you can't live a supernatural existence of total reliance on Divine Providence without making some kind of effort." The mountain of gold alludes to perfect trust in Hashem, a level of complete freedom from monetary lust. At this level, one need not lift a finger to make a living. The greater the emuna, the more one's subsistence arrives automatically at one's front doorstep.

The viceroy withstands this test successfully, refusing to listen to the giant and clinging to simple emuna. He lives his simple faith that Hashem cares for the needs of every creature with compassion, above the level of nature and logic. The viceroy doesn't even need spiritual effort to make a living, for a person with perfect trust in Hashem receives his livelihood without even having to pray.

A Place in the World to Come

The principle test of a person's emuna is in the area of income and making a living. Our sages teach that whoever says Psalm 145 three times a day merits a place in the World to Come, for Psalm 145 reminds us of Hashem's Divine Providence, which sees to our needs every day and every hour, just as we need something. The obstacle that prevents most people from serving Hashem is the confusion about making a living. Only a person who believes that Hashem can sustain him with minimal effort on his own part can serve Hashem properly.

Now, the viceroy enjoys the strength of conviction that results from years of prayer and yearning for emuna. He has done exactly what the princess has told him to. No one can make him budge from his simple emuna, from the knowledge that there is no one or nothing other than Hashem, that His glory is everywhere, that everything is for the best, and that everything is conducted by Him in magnificent perfection. With this engraved on his mind and heart, there is no need for worry, stress, pressure, or anxiety. The main thing is to live emuna, prayer, happiness, and innocence.

Fear No One but Hashem

Dear reader, stop and think for a moment: Imagine how amazed and awed you'd be if you saw a magnificent individual that knows the entire Torah and all its secrets by heart, a miracle worker of sublime spiritual stature who controls the forces of nature. Now, imagine that he snaps his fingers, and thereby summons all the animals, the birds, and the winds whenever he desires! Then, how would you react if you saw him conversing with the animals? Imagine how impressed you'd be! Now, this same magnificent individual tells you that you are fooling yourself and that there's no way to live a life of simple emuna with no effort at all. Wouldn't you listen to him? How could you argue with someone so awesome?

Here, we must stress that true, pure, and simple emuna is so concealed that few obtain it. The giants capable of carrying the "big tree" on their shoulders – impressive rabbis, scholars of Torah, even miracle workers – although we must respect them, if they can't guide us on the sweet path of simple emuna, then they can't be our spiritual guides. We shouldn't let such "giants" scare us and deter us from the path of the true *tzaddik* that leads us to true emuna. Fear no one but Hashem.

Few people sincerely believe in the power of prayer and of emuna. Often, when they meet a person who earnestly and innocently yearns to cling to Hashem with pure and complete emuna, and lead a life of prayer and *teshuva*, they chide him and ridicule his emuna. "*Hitbodedut*? Who do you think you are, the Baal Shem Tov? Who needs it? The important thing is to learn Torah and make a living. Get those weird ideas out of your head! That's not for you! You can't cling to Hashem with pure emuna – that's impossible!"

Retired Chassidim

Our holy Rebbe Nachman said that there are those that set out to serve Hashem, but later became discouraged. When these people see others who truly yearn to serve Hashem with earnest, praying at length and with enthusiasm, they make fun of them and try to weaken them. These "retired Chassidim" who have fallen by the spiritual wayside can't stand to see others striving to serve Hashem.

Tenacity

The viceroy clings to emuna and cries bitterly when he hears the heresy that questions the truth. He's tenacious and firm in his belief that there's a path to simple emuna that's open to everyone on every spiritual level.

As soon as a person desires to live by the advice and guidance of the true *tzaddik*, he arouses a mountain of resistance from within and from without. One must be tenacious, clinging to his faith in the true *tzaddik* with no reservations. If the *tzaddik* says we can reach the level of simple and pure emuna, it must be true! We must therefore fulfill the directives of the *tzaddik* in their entirety, just as Rebbe Nathan so meticulously followed everything Rebbe Nachman said with complete dedication, no matter how much other people – both family and strangers – hampered him. Even the opposition of Rebbe Nathan's father-in-law, one of the greatest rabbinical authorities of his generation, couldn't deter him from implementing every iota of Rebbe Nachman's advice. After every lesson that Rebbe Nathan heard from Rebbe Nachman, he'd run to the forest and pray all night long that he'd be able to internalize and implement everything that he had learned. For that reason, he achieved what other disciples of Rebbe Nachman did not.

We see that once the viceroy was tenacious and steadfast in his convictions, then even the giant became submissive and helped him. Once again, we see the principle that if a person is strong and believes in what he's doing, then the hindrances become assisting agents. With true and strong emuna, one's parents, spouse, and even great rabbis will fall at his feet and come to his aid.

Chapter Thirteen

One Obstacle after Another

S o the giant said to him, "I think it is nonsense. But since you persist, I am in charge of the animals. I will do this for you: I will call them all. For they traverse the whole world, perhaps one of them will know where the mountain and the castle are." And he called them all, from the smallest to the largest, all the varieties of animals, and asked them. And all of them answered that they had not seen these things. So he said, "You see that they told you nonsense. If you want my advice, turn back, because you certainly will not find it, for it does not exist..."

go around

hard to overcome

Although the viceroy has overcome the obstacle of the giant, he's now faced with another formidable obstacle, since the animals have circumvented the globe and now report that they've seen no mountain of gold and castle of pearls. But, once again, the viceroy is neither deterred nor confused; with clarity of thought, he remains committed to his firm convictions. As such, even the obstacle becomes a source of assistance, for the giant decides to help the viceroy in his search for the princess.

A nd he pleaded passionately with him, saying, "But it absolutely must exist!" So the giant said to him, "Behold, in this desert also lives my brother, and he is in charge of the birds. Perhaps they know, since they fly at great heights - perhaps they saw this mountain and castle. Go to him and tell him that I sent you to him." So he searched for him for several years...

The viceroy continues on his way, but this time, he makes a mistake: Instead of searching for the princess, he is searching for the giant's brother. Such a mistake can be tragic; once a person develops a connection to a true *tzaddik*, he or she shouldn't seek advice from others. The giant already tried to discourage the viceroy from continuing the search altogether. By a miracle, the viceroy summoned the inner strength and self composure to do what he knew was right, despite the apparent proof and arguments to the contrary. If the giant almost succeeded in convincing the viceroy to abort the search, then why is the viceroy now searching for the giant's brother? Who's to say whether he'll be able to withstand another test of faith?

equivalent

Therefore, one should never accept advice from or depend on those who don't lead him on the path of the true *tzaddik*. Rebbe Nachman explains that only the true *tzaddik* can give complete and proper advice (see Likutei Moharan I:7): "It's impossible to arrive at truth without getting close to *tzaddikim* and walking in the path of their advice. The advice one receives from them is spiritually tantamount to a marital bond. How does advice resemble the marital bond? Advice comes from the kidneys (see Gemara, tractate Shabbat 61), and the kidneys are also vessels of the seed and tools of giving birth. As such, when a person receives advice from someone, it's like receiving the seed of that person, whether he is righteous or wicked. The advice of the *tzaddik* is totally the seed of truth…"

And again he found a very large man, as before. He was also carrying a massive tree, as before. And this giant also asked him as had the first. And he told him the whole story, and that his brother had sent him to him. This giant also discouraged him, saying that it certainly did not exist. And he pleaded with him as with the first. Then the giant said to him, "Behold, I am in charge of the birds; I will call them, perhaps they know." So he called all the birds, and asked them all, from the smallest to the largest, and they answered that they did

not know anything about this mountain and castle. So the giant said to him, "You see, it certainly does not exist. If you want my advice, turn back, for it simply does not exist." But he pleaded with him, saying "It certainly exists..."

The events of the viceroy's encounter with the first giant now repeat themselves in the encounter with the giant's brother. The latter, willfully or not, also tries to discourage the viceroy from continuing the innocent search for the princess, or true and complete emuna. This is what happens when a person seeks advice from others, rather than depending on the advice of the *tzaddik* with simple and pure faith.

Fortunately, the viceroy's self composure and strength of conviction come to his aid. He knows what he has to do and he knows that the princess's instructions are absolute truth. If she said to search for a mountain of gold and castle of pearls, then there's no doubt whatsoever that they exist! This strength of conviction gives the viceroy power to continue and to stand on what he knows is right, and once again, the obstacle becomes an aid. Everything takes a turn for the best. Then, as another test of faith, things turn for the worst, for the birds know nothing about a mountain of gold and castle of pearls. Once again, the viceroy doesn't budge from his stance of truth – he shatters the obstacle and the giant's brother now becomes a source of assistance, and sends the viceroy to a third brother. This time, the viceroy focuses on his search for the princess, and not on his search for outside help; as such, he succeeds!

The second giant said to him, "Further ahead in the desert lives my brother, who is in charge of the winds, and they run around the whole world. Perhaps they know." So he went several more years searching, and found also this giant, who was also carrying a giant tree. And the giant asked him, as the others had. And he told him the whole story, as before. And the giant discouraged him, as before. And

> he pleaded with him as well. So the third giant said to him, that for his sake he would call all the winds and ask them. He called them, and all the winds came, and he asked them all, and not one of them knew about the mountain and the castle. So the giant said to him, "You see, they told you nonsense." And the viceroy began to cry bitterly, and said, "I *know* that it certainly exists..."

This is the first time that the viceroy says the words, "I **know** that it certainly exists." His emuna, in attaining the level of firm knowledge, marks the beginning of the *geula*, or the redemption of emuna.

> **A**s they were speaking, one more wind came. And the giant in charge of them was annoyed with him, saying, "Why did you not come with the rest?" He answered, "I was delayed, for I needed to carry a princess to a mountain of gold and a castle of pearls." And the viceroy was overjoyed...

Why did the last wind wait until now to carry the princess to the mountain of gold and castle of pearls? Several years have transpired since she told the viceroy that she'd be there. Where was she all these years? We see that only after the viceroy attained the level of firm and complete emuna - having withstood countless trials, tribulations, difficulties, and setbacks – only then did the princess arrive at the place from where he could rescue her, the mountain of gold and castle of pearls. The redemption of emuna depends solely on our efforts in this lowly physical world. One's personal *geula* depends on one's dedicated hard work, which takes emuna out from exile and hastens the *geula* of the entire world.

> **T**he one in charge asked the wind, "What is expensive there? (In other words, what

things are considered valuable and important there?)" He answered him, "Everything there is extremely expensive..."

As we learned earlier, the mountain of gold and the castle of pearls allude to monetary lust. Where there's monetary lust, emuna is in exile. The viceroy must journey to this place of monetary lust in order to rescue and redeem the princess. Since the princess is captive in a place of monetary lust, then the question that the giant in charge asks is quite understandable: "What is expensive there?" He receives the answer that everything is expensive there. Surely, wherever there's monetary lust, everything is very expensive, for people there crave making more and more money. Another interpretation is that in a place where there's emuna, everything is precious (*the Hebrew word for expensive and precious is identical, "yakar"*).

So the one in charge of the winds said to the viceroy, "Seeing that you have been searching for her such a long time, and you went through many difficulties. Perhaps now you will be hindered by expenses. Therefore I am giving you this vessel. Every time you reach into it, you will receive money from it..."

Here we see how the third giant – who was an obstacle at first – does an about-face to the extent that he offers to remove further obstacles from the viceroy's path. In other words, not only has he stopped trying to discourage the viceroy, but now he's willing to help. He offers to cover all the viceroy's expenses and assure that there won't be additional obstacles in the viceroy's path.

Here, we learn a remarkable lesson in life of just how powerful the yearning, desire, and tenacity for holiness are. Nothing compares with walking steadfast in the path of pure, innocent, and simple emuna. When a person clings to the path of innocent faith with strength, even the greatest barriers become agents of assistance;

not only that, but they protect the faithful from further obstacles.

The viceroy receives a vessel in which he merely inserts his hand, and withdraws whatever money he needs. The vessel is symbolic of the level of *bitachon*, or complete trust in Hashem. The viceroy worked and strived for this level, having shattered any lust for money while acquiring emuna and perfect trust that Hashem alone sustains and feeds every creature on earth. Now, he has the complete trust that Hashem will give him whatever he needs for Divine service, no matter what the sum. He doesn't have the slightest doubt that he'll get whatever he needs whenever he needs it.

Our holy Rebbe Nachman teaches (Likutei Moharan, I:60), that there's a level of observation in Torah that requires a high level of opulence. In other words, that one who attains such a level must have unlimited funds. Therefore, the worthy person of this particular spiritual level is granted unlimited riches from above. Any needs that a person requires for his service of Hashem are fulfilled. This is the opulence of holiness, which means that a person receives all the money in the world if he needs it for his learning and understanding of Torah. The viceroy attained this level by virtue of his dedicated hard work, receiving this particular vessel to enable him to rescue the princess with ease.

A nd he commanded the aforementioned wind to take him there. The storm wind came, and carried him there...

According to Jewish esoteric thought, the "storm wind" is one of the three *kelipot*, or strong spirits of impurity. Once again, we witness the fact that when a person stubbornly walks the path of righteousness and truth, even the *Sitra Achra* helps him redeem emuna.

...and brought him to the gate. There were guards posted there, that would not let him enter the city. So he reached into the vessel, took out money and bribed them...

Since the princess is captive in a place of monetary lust, then with money, the viceroy can do whatever he wants and bribe whomever he wants. When a person has a certain lust, particularly the lust for money, he or she can be easily bribed and blinded by the object of their lust, for the Torah says that a bribe can even blind the eyes of the wise (see Devarim, ch. 16).

We see clearly how lust, particularly monetary lust, clouds and distorts a person's judgment. He or she is incapable of accepting or listening to anything that incompatible with their lust. Such people certainly don't want to hear that they are living a lie; indeed, they *can't* hear or see the error of their ways.

Money especially is a test of faith, as our sages said (Gemara, tractate Eruvin 65): "Three things characterize a person – his goblet, his purse, and his anger." In other words, a person's character is evident by how he acts when drinking wine, when dealing with money, and when encountering a challenge to his temper.

Another allusion to one's behavior in monetary matters appears in the Mishna (tractate Zevachim, ch. 5): "The holy of holy sacrifices are slaughtered in the north." In other words, if you want to examine if a person is really as "holy of holies" as he presents himself, slaughter him in the "north", for "north" symbolizes money. You can check a person's true character by testing him in financial matters. Is he fair in commerce? Does he give to charity? Does he pay his workers on time? Does he adhere to the laws of Torah that tell him when and how to spend money? Does he avoid touching a cent that doesn't belong to him? If the answer to all these questions is yes, then that person truly is "holy of holies." So, when you slaughter him in his "north" – you take away his money – then he'll show just how much genuine emuna he really has.

> **...and entered the city. And it was a beautiful city. He approached a man, and rented lodgings, for he would need to stay there some time. For it would need much cunning and wisdom to free her...**

Again, we see just how much patience we need in redeeming emuna. Even now – after the viceroy has attained lofty spiritual levels and traversed a myriad of obstacles – he has reached the place where he can free the princess, but he still must wait. The task of waiting is a lofty spiritual task, required at every rung of the spiritual ladder. Mistakes and blemishes come from haste and impatience, like picking unripe fruit: Today, it's sour. But if one waits for the right time a few days later, the same fruit will be delightfully sweet. Even great *tzaddikim* have made the mistake – relative to their lofty spiritual status, of course – of trying to hasten the premature. Hashem has His own time table of salvations.

Hashem alone did, does, and will do every action in the universe. Our task is simply to desire to fulfill Hashem's will, and to yearn with pangs of longing for the moment when we can do His bidding. When the right time comes, Hashem helps a person to successfully complete his task and to merit a fulfilling life of Torah, mitzvot, and good deeds.

And how he freed her, he did not tell, but in the end he freed her...

Rebbe Nachman didn't reveal how the viceroy freed the princess, for it's impossible to tell – this is a personal story that varies from person to person. Each one of us has to rescue his or her own personal princess – emuna – and reveal emuna to the world. Each person has his or her own way of accomplishing this task, and one person can't imitate another's method, for each soul has its own mission and mode of operation. There's no connection at all between one person's way of serving Hashem and another person's.

For that reason, it's senseless to look at other people. Each of us is a unique individual with a unique task that no one else can do. Rebbe Nachman elaborates on the passage in Ezekiel, Chapter 33, that states, "Abraham was one." Abraham served Hashem as if he were the only person in the world, and therefore ignored all the idolaters all around him.

Just as every individual has a separate genetic map, each soul has its own spiritual root, task, and *tikkun* in the world. For that reason, there's no purpose in judging ourselves by comparing ourselves with others. For example, if one person learns four hours of Gemara in one sitting, but another person's attention span, especially for Gemara, is half an hour, that doesn't mean that the latter is inferior, Heaven forbid. It could be that he has already corrected what he needed to correct in the area of Talmudic study in a previous reincarnation, while during this life, his mission is totally different. No one expects a fisherman to fly a jet aircraft. Conversely, a jet pilot can't sell you a fish for your Shabbat meal. Each of us has his or her own vital mission. Therefore, we should concentrate on performing our task with joy and innocence no matter how Hashem runs our lives without comparing ourselves to anyone else, for Hashem leads each of us down the path that is conducive to our own individual *tikkun*.

helpful

Confession

The only way to find our unique path in life and in the service of Hashem – without confusion and without becoming discouraged from looking at and listening to others – is to spend an hour a day in *hitbodedut*, personal prayer and self-evaluation. Rebbe Nachman explains (see Likutei Moharan I: 4), that when a person confesses daily, then the true *tzaddik* helps pave the way to a true correction of the soul according to that individual's needs. When Rebbe Nachman was alive, his disciples would confess to him personally. Now that Rebbe Nachman is no longer in the flesh, we confess in our personal prayer to Hashem, and we maintain our bond with our teacher and spiritual guide - Rebbe Nachman – by fulfilling his directives and advice as brought down in his writings. When we do so, Rebbe Nachman intervenes on our behalf in the upper worlds, and from his sphere of influence there – unlimited by physical boundaries and restraints – and helps each of us that is bound to him. The Gemara teaches us that the true *tzaddik* never dies, and can do much more after his life in the material world than he can during his physical existence.

In addition, *hitbodedut* is the only thing in the service of Hashem that is truly personal. All other mitzvot are mostly standard and uniform: Everyone wears tefillin, everyone learns Torah, and everyone observes the Sabbath. Everyone even prays from the same prescribed prayers.

Only *hitbodedut* is totally individual; there are no ironclad laws and no standard format. Each person pours his heart out to Hashem according to his current state of mind and body. This is the place to emphasize and warn that no one must hear what we say to Hashem. If someone has the urge to yell or cry out, he or she must be absolutely certain that no one else is within earshot. One can also cry out in silence, from the depths of the heart. Such a silent scream can't even be heard by the person sitting next to you on the train or plane.

Therefore, our holy Rebbe didn't tell us how the viceroy freed the princess, for the way to free the princess is by way of *hitbodedut*, which varies from person to person. If someone truly yearns for emuna and to rescue his own personal princess, then he should devote an hour a day to *hitbodedut*, no matter what.

Thoughts of Repentance

Now, we can readily understand what our holy Rebbe Nachman said in the introduction: "Along the way, I told a tale, that everyone who heard it had thoughts of repentance…" *keen*

When a person merits hearing this poignant tale of the lost princess, and sees the viceroy's dedication in finding and freeing her, the perseverance, conviction, commitment, yearning, and triumph over all obstacles and setbacks – even when the princess becomes more elusive – he or she is aroused with a desire for *teshuva*, for getting closer to Hashem. The road to *teshuva* is strewn with obstacles, barriers, setbacks, highs and lows, successes and failures. Likewise, when we walk the path of *teshuva* with the same courage and conviction that the viceroy exhibited in the performance of his challenging task, we're assured ultimate success. The important thing is to constantly fuel the desire and yearning for holiness at all costs, forever continuing our personal search for true emuna.

This is the thought of repentance – arousing the strong desire to walk in the path of *teshuva*, no matter what, saying in our hearts, "I want to make *teshuva*! I'll never abandon my desire to get close to Hashem!

Completed with Hashem's loving grace, may His Holy Name be praised forever and ever

Glossary

Amalek (Biblical) – evil grandson of Esau; nickname for the *Yetzer Hara*, the Evil Inclination

Baal Teshuva (Hebrew) – spiritually awakened Jew

Bitul (Hebrew) – literally "cancellation;" in spirituality, it connotes the nullification of ego necessary for willful submission to a higher authority.

Chassid (Hebrew) – literally "pious person", but alludes to the disciples of the Chassidic movement, founded by Rabbi Yisroel Baal Shem Tov in the early 18th Century CE

Dinim (Hebrew) – the spiritual forces of severe judgments that are created by a person's misdeeds.

Emuna (Hebrew) - the firm belief in a single, supreme, omniscient, benevolent, spiritual, supernatural, and all-powerful Creator of the universe, who we refer to as God.

Emunat Chachamim (Hebrew) - the belief in our sages

Gemara (Aramaic) – The 2nd-5th Century CE elaborations on the Mishna, which serve as the foundation of Jewish law

Geula (Hebrew) – the redemption process of the Jewish people

Hashem (Hebrew) - literally means "the name", a substitute term for The Almighty so that we don't risk using God's name in vain.

Hashgacha Pratit (Hebrew) – Divine Providence, Hashem's individual and personal supervision over each creation

Hitbodedut (Hebrew) – personal prayer, usually in seclusion

Kabbala (Hebrew) - Jewish esoteric thought

Kedusha (Hebrew) – holiness

Kelim (Hebrew) – literally tools or vessels, in Kabbala these are the vessels that hold Divine illumination

Malchut (Hebrew) – monarchy, the 7th lower sphere of Divinity in Kabbalistic thought

Mishna (Hebrew) – The oral elaboration of the Torah as given from Hashem to Moses, finally codified by Rabbi Akiva, his pupil Rabbi Meir, and his pupil Rabbi Yehuda HaNassi, 1st-2nd Century, CE

Mitzvah (Hebrew) – a commandment of the Torah; good deed.

Mitzvot (Hebrew, pl.) – literally, the commandments of the Torah; good deeds.

Moshiach (Hebrew) – Messiah

Neshama (Hebrew) – a person's Divine soul

Ratzon (Hebrew) – will, desire

Shabbat (Hebrew) – Sabbath, day of rest

Shalom Bayit (Hebrew) – literally "peace in the home", marital bliss

Shmirat Habrit (Hebrew) – literally "guarding the covenant"; male holiness in thought, speech, and deed, particularly the use of one's reproductive organs only in the performance of a mitzvah

Shmirat Eynayim (Hebrew) – "guarding the eyes", or refraining from looking at forbidden objects, particularly at a woman other than one's wife

Shulchan Aruch (Hebrew) – Code of Jewish Law, compiled by Rabbi Joseph Caro of Tzfat, late 16th Century CE

Sitra Achra (Aramaic) – literally "the dark side", connotes the forces of evil, the opposite of holiness

Shmitta – Sabbatical year, once every seven years when the land is allowed to rest

Talmud (Hebrew) – Jewish oral tradition, comprised of the Mishna and the Gemara

Tanna (Aramaic) – Mishnaic sage, 1st – 2nd Century CE

Tikkun (Hebrew)   correction of the soul

Tikkunim (Hebrew) – plural for tikkun

Teshuva (Hebrew) – literally "returning", the term that refers to the process of atoning for one's misdeeds

Tzaddik (Hebrew) – extremely pious and upright person

Tzaddikim (Hebrew) – plural for *tzaddik*

Tzedaka (Hebrew) – charity

Yetzer Hara (Hebrew) – Evil Inclination

Yetzer Tov (Hebrew) – inclination to do good

Yir'at Shamayim (Hebrew) – literally "the fear of Hashem", a term for sincere piety

Zohar (Hebrew) - the 2nd-Century C.E. esoteric interpretation of the Torah by Rebbe Shimon Bar Yochai and his disciples

Did you enjoy this book?

If so, please help us spread the message of emuna around the world. Send your contributions to:

Chut Shel Chesed POB 50226 Jerusalem, Israel

Or call:
Brooklyn: 718-577-2975
Los Angeles: 323-271-0581
Israel: 972-57-31-26441